TYRONE SMITH

OUTSIDE
the
HUDDLE

Steps to Developing a Game Plan for Life

EQUIP **24** SEVEN

Outside the Huddle – Steps to Developing a Game Plan for Life by Tyrone Smith

Copyright © 2016 by Tyrone Smith

E Q U I P 24 S E V E N

Equip 24/7
Post Office Box 941176
Houston, Texas 77094

Front cover photo by Chap Edmonson
Back cover photo by Jonathan Daniels
Cover design by Panagiotis Lampridis
Interior design by Glenn Bontrager at Sarco Press
Edited by Erica L. James
Publisher: Equip 24 Seven

Visit the author's website at www.tyronesmith24.com

For more information about special discounts for bulk purchases, please contact Equip 24 Seven Special Sales:
(713) 571-9121 or info@tyronesmith24.com

First Edition: September 2016
Printed in the United States of America.
Library of Congress Control Number: 2016906653
ISBN 978-0985786700

DEDICATION

This is book dedicated to my family for all of the continued loved and support through the years. The reason I am the person that I am today is because of your support and encouragement throughout my life. Your love has strengthened me and enabled me to reach beyond myself to make a difference in the lives of others.

TABLE OF CONTENTS

"It begins by building each individual and helping them see the greatness inside of themselves. By helping others to unlock their own possibilities, we are creating better opportunities for our world."

– *Tyrone Smith*

OUTSIDE
the
HUDDLE

Steps to Developing a Game Plan for Life

FOREWORD

NFL players are elite athletes, to say the least. Usually from childhood to adulthood, they live their developmental years *in the huddle* with teammates whose friendships are forged in the fires of the gridiron. At a young age, they are taught to live and breathe beneath the Friday night lights. In each of their minds is etched the notion that grueling practices, scrimmages, spring training and preseason workouts are what determine the success of the competitor. As early as the player can remember, there in the stands are both professional and amateur scouts making predictions about their football futures. Each aspiring football player works diligently to win the ultimate prize of competing at the highest level of competition: Sunday, Monday Night and Thursday Night Football. However, there is a game more valuable than the ultimate team sport; it is the game of life. That game is won, in the words of Tyrone Smith, "*Outside the Huddle.*"

I had the pleasure of watching Tyrone compete as a high

school athlete, collegiate athlete, and professional athlete. With each level of play, he always played to win. He was successful because he worked hard to prepare himself both mentally and physically, and then incorporated that work ethic on game day. Tyrone taught me that the practice field is where the game is actually won, during the times when no fans are watching. That mentality earned him the respect of his teammates on the field, and now continues to earn him the respect of others off the field. As much as I enjoyed watching Tyrone succeed at the game of football, the game I enjoy watching him succeed in now is the game of life.

To watch Tyrone excel as an unapologetic Christian father, husband, community leader and minister to youth is a sight to behold. In this book, Tyrone brings to bear all of the teachings he has learned from his parents, coexisting with his siblings, teachers, coaches, mentors and his pastor. He combines all of what he has accumulated throughout his journey into a solid practical approach on how to play the game of life and win. I have known Tyrone for over 20 years and I have watched him win some of life's toughest battles. In this book, Tyrone lays out a strategic game plan for life. Like the football games he played, he teaches you how to take the game to your opponents and win!

Dr. Ralph Douglas West
Brookhollow Baptist Church
Senior Pastor

LETTERS FROM FORMER STUDENTS

Tyrone Smith has had a positive impact on my life. I have had the opportunity to participate in his camps as a student and as a counselor. Each experience has been a great one, and I always learned something new about myself and about life. Life is unpredictable, and you never know what life will throw at you. Through Mr. Smith, I have learned to accept the good and the bad because there is always a lesson that you can learn from each. You have to learn to adapt and to be flexible, because everything in life won't go as you had planned.

Mr. Smith has always taught me to love myself and to believe in myself. You can't expect others to believe in you if you don't believe in yourself. You will fail at times, and that's okay. Failure is a part of growing and reaching your goals that you have set for yourself. Every time you fail, you get back up and try again. Mr. Smith has taught me to expect nothing but the best from myself, and nothing less. If you have a goal, or a dream, go for it! Push yourself, and reach for it! Mr. Smith has truly been an inspiration when it comes to reaching my dreams. I don't know what the rest of my life has for me, but I do know that I want success, and, I want to be a better person than I was yesterday. I believe that everyone has a purpose, and our purpose is our destiny.

I thank Mr. Smith from the bottom of my heart for everything he has done, everything he's doing, and everything he will do in the future. If he has touched my life, I know he has touched many more lives as well. He is a great role model, very humble, a leader, and a man of God.

Chelsea Davis

* * * * * ● * * * * *

I was introduced to Tyrone Smith and his team when I registered for a program called the Journey Beyond Dreams College Experience Program in 2003 as a high school junior. The program was designed to expose first generation, inner city students to the college experience, and for me this was the first time I ever stepped foot on a college campus.

At the time, the program seemed to just be an opportunity for a "free trip." In reality, it was the moment that changed my own perspective on my future. During the two weeks we participated in workshops and group activities, led by Tyrone Smith, which empowered me to believe that

I could achieve my goals and be successful at anything I set my mind to.

After the Journey Beyond Dreams College Experience Program and graduating high school, I attended Sam Houston State University and earned a Bachelor's in Business Administration and continued to earn my Master's in Public Service and Administration from Texas A&M.

I was fortunate to have had the opportunity to work many summers as a staff member in different camps and as an intern with First and Goal, Inc. the summer of 2009. These opportunities provided me with a new perspective on the hard work and dedication Tyrone Smith has towards making a difference in the lives of students. This also allowed me to see the positive impact his programs have on students, their families, and their futures.

His programs not only changed the outlook of my own life, but also have impacted the lives of many more. I will forever be grateful to have had the opportunity to meet Tyrone more than 10 years ago, but also for his giving me the opportunity to work with him and help him in his mission.

Today, I live by something he taught me, and something I consistently tell my students: "Success is a journey, not a destination. And it doesn't matter where you start, but it's about where you finish."

Tyrone, thank you for everything you have done and

continue to do. The world is a better place thanks to your work and your continued service to our youth.

Maggie Manzano

· · · · **·** · · · ·

As kids everybody asks the question, "Who do you want to be like when you grow up?" During my childhood I heard that many times, although I never really paid that much attention to it. It's been eight years, almost nine, since I came to the United States, and that same question has always followed me (although I've encountered a few people who I have said I'd like to be like). During the summer of my junior year in high school, I had the privilege to attend the "Journey Beyond Dreams" program sponsored by First and Goal, Inc.

One of the main mentors in this program was Tyrone Smith. He had a great team that helped me open my eyes to the countless opportunities that I had before me in life. As time passed, Tyrone Smith, the image of someone who worked many hours and gave 110% in everything he did, impacted my life tremendously. Tyrone Smith and his team increased my desire to be someone in life; as of today, I am in my third year of college, and I've accomplished many things that I would have never thought I could do. This is possible because of the individuals from that program that influenced me for the better.

For years I have kept in contact with Mr. Smith, hoping that one day he would give me an opportunity to be a part of his team and to make an impact like he does for others. Because of all of the help and opportunities that I've encountered and being in the right place at the right moments, I am where I am today; it has transformed my mentality. Today I can answer the question I was asked many times as a kid, "Who do you want to be like when you grow up?" One of the answers would be Mr. Smith. From him I learned that I should help others and inspire them to continue to follow their dreams, like I was inspired to follow mine by many people, including Tyrone Smith.

Hector Marquez

. . . . . ● . . . . .

Tyrone Smith once shared the story about the "World's Smartest Man" and asked all of the students what did the world's smartest man have in his hands. He stated . . . "that bird's life lies in your hands." Except it wasn't a bird; it was my life, and I have control over it. I've always approached life on the sidelines and let my actions speak for themselves. I wasn't much of a vocal leader until the *Prepare to Dream College Experience Program* in 2008 at the University of Texas. Tyrone took the group through a series of leadership and skill building exercises that awoke a voice inside of me. I could either lead or be led. I chose the former. The wise man in my story was Tyrone and everyone involved with First and Goal, Inc. I've since graduated from the University of Texas at Austin with a Bachelor's Degree in Journalism and now live in New York. I'm nowhere near where I want to be in life, but I know as long as I continue to remember who is in control I can do anything I set my mind to.

Roman Coronado

LETTER FROM MY COACH

I met Tyrone Smith when I was a young coach at Christa McAuliffe Middle School. Tyrone was in the 8th grade, and I coached him in football and in track. I don't know how Tyrone and I got so attached to each other. I believe it was the Spirit of God. He was very quiet, he worked harder than anyone else, and you could tell that he wanted to make something out of himself. He attended our Fellowship of Christian Athletes meetings, where he grew spiritually as a young man. He was one of my hurdlers, and I frequently would take him home because his parents worked a lot. During that time, I would give him advice and you could tell that he was listening intently. We talked about life, decision-making, goals; we talked about a little bit of everything. When he graduated to high school, a year later I was promoted to coach and teacher at the high school he was attending, Willowridge High School. From Christa McAuliffe Middle School, to Willowridge High School, to Baylor University, to the San Francisco 49ers, to marriage, to the present, I have always been in his life to train him or to give him advice. When he started First and Goal, Inc. and he mentioned how he wanted to make a difference in the lives of kids by starting a mentoring program, I was amazed at how GOD had transformed this quiet kid to an amazing man of GOD! He often would thank me for being in his life and mentoring him. However, he didn't know how much he helped me to find my purpose in life. He actually helped me because I was lost and didn't know if my life had a purpose. I wanted to be more than just a coach and a teacher, but also a man who made a difference in the lives of others. Every time I hear of Tyrone's accomplishments, or when I see him with his family and all the things he is doing to help others, I thank GOD for letting me have a small part in the life of this great man.

Anyone who reads his book will be inspired to believe that they can do all things and accomplish great things!

Sincerely,
Dennis Brantley
Head Football Coach/Campus Athletic Coordinator
Elkins HS

LETTER FROM MY MENTOR

In 1990, after playing eight seasons as a running back in the NFL, I decided to retire at the ripe old age of 32. Having been an athlete all my life, I was uncertain as to what I would do for a second career in this new phase of my life. I returned to my hometown of Waco, Texas to continue my education in graduate school at my alma mater, Baylor University.

After completing graduate school, I obtained a job as an academic counselor for student-athletes. My greatest desire was to help young athletes earn their degrees. I wanted them to avoid the pitfalls of focusing too much on their sport and not enough on their education. I knew many players in the NFL who had fallen into that category. I wanted to share my knowledge and experiences with the student-athletes at Baylor to help adequately prepare them for the day they walked away from the game.

Tyrone Smith was one of the athletes assigned to me during his freshman year. I could tell immediately that he was different from the other freshman athletes I had experienced in my role as a counselor. As a student, Tyrone possessed a level of maturity beyond his years. During each of our weekly counseling sessions, he was punctual, engaging, and inquisitive. He listened intently to the advice I shared with him.

Our conversations were not solely focused on academics and football. He talked passionately about his family, his love for God, and his goals in life. Beneath his words, I sensed an intense determination to succeed no matter what path he chose to pursue. For the next four years, I watched Tyrone improve as a player and grow as a person. I was inspired to witness his success on the field and in the classroom. When Tyrone left Baylor and joined the San Francisco 49ers football club, he would occasionally return to Waco and pay me a visit.

During each of his visits, he would make it a point to thank me for believing in him and for encouraging him to be the best he could be. Although he credits me with having a positive influence in his life, it was his own internal drive and moral compass that propelled him to the success he is experiencing in his life.

This book will be an inspiration to all who read it. Tyrone's life journey is compelling. It illustrates that our environment does not define us. We are defined by the choices we make, by the people with whom we choose to surround ourselves, and by our ability to discover our true purpose. Tyrone gives us the keys to developing a plan to find that purpose.

While I treasure my friendship with Tyrone, that relationship is not the sole reason I recommend this book. I encourage you to read it because it is based on valid principles that I have utilized in my own life. It has been said that success is not measured solely by how high you climb the ladder of success, but by the number of people you help to climb that ladder. Tyrone has helped thousands of young people by giving each of them the basic steps to begin their climb to a successful future. Although an injury played a significant role in Tyrone's decision to leave football behind, it took a tremendous amount of courage for him to do so. I admire him for believing in himself and for charting such a glowing path for others to follow.

If you are a young person wanting to find your true purpose in life, or if you are a caring mom, dad, or coach looking for a practical, easy-to-understand resource, this book is for you. Read **Outside the Huddle: Steps to Developing a Game Plan for Life** and begin your own personal journey to success by discovering your true purpose.

Walter Abercrombie, M.S. Ed.
Executive Director
"B" Association, Baylor University
Former NFL Running Back

INTRODUCTION

· · · · · ● · · · ·

We all have a purpose for existing that goes beyond ourselves. My reason for writing *Outside the Huddle* is to help others by sharing the lessons that I have learned during my journey to discover my true life's purpose. My journey led me to the knowledge that my reason for existence extended far beyond the game of football.

This book will identify eight key principles to help individuals thrive, not just survive. Throughout this book, you will learn how to use and apply these practical principles to your life. *Outside the Huddle: Steps to Developing a Game Plan for Life* focuses on ways for individuals to get the most out of their talents and skills, and apply them in everyday situations.

In *Outside the Huddle*, I share the personal stories that shaped me into the person that I am today. These stories go beyond the game of football to show both on-the-field and off-the-field perspectives regarding some of the most important moments of my life. I can truly say that the game of football has shaped my life in monumental ways. Through football, I learned the importance of discipline, commitment, teamwork, and perseverance. However, the moments that have had the greatest impact on my life and that have helped me develop a greater understanding of who I am happened *off the field.*

In order to make one's dreams, aspirations, and goals a reality, it is necessary to develop a game plan. *Outside the Huddle* will address ways that individuals can develop a plan of action for reaching their dreams. I will share fundamental steps and principles that I have lived by and that have helped me create my own success story. While living by the principles outlined in *Outside the Huddle*, I have been able to uncover my true purpose: making a difference in the lives of others. I believe that the same principles will help others discover their purpose and live more successful, fulfilled lives.

What is success?

If you ask five people what it means to be successful, more than likely you will receive five different answers. This is because success means something different to each of us. For some, success means financial gains, reveling in luxuries and accumulating material possessions. For others, it means having a position of power and status within a community, profession, or organization. Others believe success means being content with who you are and who others perceive you to be.

In writing *Outside the Huddle*, it is not my intention to tell you that your definition of success is right or wrong. I have followed a path created by certain principles during my journey toward success, and I want to share the principles that I have learned along the way. In this book, I explain my growing up as an inner city youth deemed "at-risk" to the drugs, crime, and violence of my community; I also tell about becoming a professional football player and dealing with the on and off the field pressures associated with that industry; and finally, I explain my choice to leave the sport that I loved to fulfill my true purpose of mentoring children and young adults. I have been given a unique perspective on what success in life means. However, the eight principles in this book should not be seen as a systematic checklist to becoming successful. Rather, the eight "Power Principles" outlined here are the key elements drawn from lessons throughout my life that have helped me create my path to success. I hope that sharing my experiences will help you in your journey toward success, and will help you define success for your life.

Tyrone Smith

OUTSIDE
the
HUDDLE

Steps to Developing a Game Plan for Life

PURPOSE

· · · · · ● · · · ·

"The only one who can tell you 'you can't' is you.
And you don't have to listen."

-Nike

There will be moments when you will reflect on the life you have lived and think deeply about the future. There also will be moments when you will realize, sometimes with little notice, what it is that you are destined to do. When this moment arrives, you should be prepared to appreciate this moment of realization for what it truly is: an opportunity to be true to yourself. Here is my moment of truth.

I sat down on the bench, ignoring the way that it creaked

and moaned as I shifted my weight to find a comfortable position. I closed my eyes, willing my body to take a moment to rest. I relished the feel of the cool, concrete wall as I leaned my back against it. Head bowed, earphones on, I focused on the rhythm and lyrics pouring from my CD player. My head bobbed to the beat as I listened to the sermon that Tupac Shakur was preaching to me. "Lord, I suffered through the years and shed so many tears." His words were preparing me for battle. His music had become my game day ritual. It was all that I listened to on game days; it was the only song on the CD that I listened to repeatedly.

I had an instant connection to Tupac's "Shed So Many Tears" the first time that I heard the words. I had heard the song so many times that when I closed my eyes I saw each line of the song clearly, as though the words were imprinted on the inside of my eyelids. It was my anthem. I felt an ache inside the lyrics, a sorrow born from the deep regret of the songwriter for his unfulfilled dreams and his longing for hopes that had died long ago. I recognized the wretched images of dreams deferred and what my own life would have been if I had not pushed myself to keep going. I spent every waking moment desperately fighting to keep the reality of those negative images from overtaking me. However, the throbbing ache of my swollen knees and joints jolted me back to reality.

I was playing in the NFL's European League for the

Barcelona Dragons in Spain. I was having a phenomenal season—enjoying my time in a foreign country, impressing my coaches, and leading by example on and off the field while making the most out of the opportunity. My ultimate plan was to sign with another NFL team after the NFL Europe season ended.

This night I found myself sitting in a locker room so empty that the tiniest sounds were magnified as they echoed off of the walls. Two rows of fluorescent lights cast a dim yellow glow above the wooden bench. I was thankful for the solitude; it would be one of my few moments of peace before the battle ahead of me that night.

Nevertheless, my battered and bruised body protested with the slightest movement. At the age of twenty-six, I had already endured three knee surgeries. Arthritis had begun to set in from the stress of playing football since the age of twelve. Every muscle felt sore and strained to its limit. The pain was relentless. It seemed to throb in a rhythmic beat with the music. I ignored my discomfort and focused on what Tupac was preaching to me. Pain was a necessary part of the life of a warrior. I viewed my bruises as a badge of honor. I pushed the pain out of my mind; my focus was on my job. Soon other teammates arrived and began preparing for the game. I turned off my CD player as the room became charged with their energy. The moment for us to get on the field was fast approaching, and this day's battle would soon begin.

"This is what you live for," I told myself. *"This is what you were born to do."* I reminded myself of this before every game. I never wanted to take what I had for granted or forget that I was not only living my dream, but also living the dream of so many boys from my neighborhood. When you are a young, black male from an environment surrounded by poverty, making it in professional sports is the ultimate success story. I was a professional football player and I was living the dream that many young men had, but few would realize. I was lucky. No . . . I was blessed. I also knew that my family was depending on me and I did not want to disappoint them.

From the moment I stepped onto the field for that night's game, I expected that it would be more or less the same as any other. It was just another game. As in every other game, I was prepared to give it my all. I did not know at the time that I would come to give this game a special title in my life. It would be called "The Game of Purpose."

Tackle after tackle, I sent a message to everyone that no one was getting by me. In spite of my aching bones and joints, I was playing at a very high level. I was making plays all over the field. The game's commentator described my defense as "pitching a shutout," using baseball terminology to explain how well I defended my side of the field. The message that I intended to send had been received clearly. I was making hard hits with such speed and accuracy that the other team began avoiding my side of the field. The cheers of the crowd were deafening. I felt invincible—unstoppable.

It was the third down with five yards to go for the other team to make a first down, putting the team in a perfect position to score. We had to stop them with this next play. This was a huge game. Our team was our league's number one ranked defensive team, and we were playing against the league's number one ranked offensive team. The crowd yelled and screamed with an overwhelming force. This was the scoring drive that was needed for the offense (the other team) to change the fate of the game. It was a very intense moment. If we stopped the offense from getting a first down on this particular series, we were off the field so that we could rest and recover. The crowd chanted, "Let's go offense, let's go; let's go offense, let's go." As I left the defensive huddle, I focused on my assignment. In my head, I silenced the roar of the crowd to a still calm. It was time to get back to work. I felt that we had the best defensive call and scheme for this particular down. The defensive call was Easy Cover 2, one of my favorite defensive calls. Easy Cover 2 was one of the best defenses for the four wide receiver formation that the offense was running. The offense had four wide receivers in the game on this particular offensive play. I had two wide receivers aligned on my side of the field at the right corner back position. Easy Cover 2 required me to analyze both of the wide receivers' route patterns and combinations to determine how I would defend them. In the Easy Cover 2 defense, I generally anticipated that the play would come in my direction, so I was prepared to respond quickly. The first possibility in Easy Cover 2 was if the second wide receiver ran straight up the field, then I had to cover the first wide receiver man-to-man. The second possibility in Easy Cover 2 was if the second wide receiver ran a quick out route, then I had to jam the first wide receiver and proceed to hit the second wide receiver with all of my strength as he came to my area.

Then the unthinkable happened. The other team's quarterback completed a short, precise pass to the wide receiver. He was extremely fast, but I reacted quickly and ran toward him with full power. I intended for the hit to be ferocious. The impact of our contact was thunderous. Even though I had made a big play and stopped him from making the first down, I knew immediately that something was wrong. *I felt the pain that I had intended for him.* I could feel my body in an awkward position when I hit the wide receiver. The pain was sharp, shooting down my back and pulsating through my limbs. Everything felt numb, as if my limbs had instantly fallen asleep. I could not ignore the fear that I felt as my body went limp. Unable to hold my weight, I fell to the ground. Although I was surrounded by my teammates as they celebrated the play with excitement, I was alone in my misery. Unaware of my injuries, they yanked me to my feet and pounded my back and helmet, congratulating me on a great play.

My world moved in slow motion. My back and chest felt like they were on fire. The pain was excruciating. I struggled to breathe and was unable to hold back the tears that streamed down my face. *As a warrior, pain was a necessary part of your life.* Tupac's words immediately popped into my head: "Lord, I suffered through the years and shed so many tears." As if hearing my prayer, my coach took one look at me and could tell that I was in pain. My coaches called a timeout, and, somehow, I was able to make my way over to the sideline. He asked me if I was okay. Grimacing, I lied to him and said that I was fine. The opposing team was in the Red Zone—20 yards or less to the goal line—and one play away from turning it back over to our offense. I told myself that I would deal with the pain later, that the game was too important. I was a warrior.

I went back on the field hoping that the pain across my back would lessen, but it became worse with every movement. By the time I took position in front of my opponent, it was obvious that I was injured; even the wide receiver on the opposing team asked me if I was okay. I knew then that I was a liability to my team if I remained in the game. After the play, I went to the sideline and removed myself from the game.

As I headed back to the locker room, a million thoughts ran through my mind. My mind reeled with the thought of how serious my injury could be. Although the unbearable pain was an indicator that I was seriously hurt, I still held on to the hope that I would simply require a cortisone shot and would be able to return to the game. The team doctor crushed that fantasy. After he examined me, he insisted that I needed further testing and took me out of the game. Strapped to a back and neck brace, the reality of my situation began to sink in. I was terrified that my dreams might be in jeopardy, and even worse, I feared disappointing my family. My family was depending on me to make it.

That night I sat in my bed, unable to sleep. I was scheduled to see a specialist the next day, and the waiting was more than I could bear. I needed to know whether or not this was the end of my season. I arrived at the doctor's office the next day full of anxiety. During that game, I was not the only player that had been injured. One of my teammates and friends, Eddie Conti, waited alongside me. He had broken his leg and ankle in the same game. I knew that we shared the same unspoken fears that our injuries could be career ending. He was nearly inconsolable in his anxiety. I focused on him, not wanting to see a friend in such distress. I continually told him that his life was bigger than the game of football, and although I spoke those words to him, I knew that it was a message that I needed to receive. While we were waiting, I encouraged and prayed with him. As we prayed, I found my own inner peace to accept whatever verdict I would receive that day. The doctor called him in before me, and I continued to pray for him. When he came out he shared his good news. The doctors had told him that he would need surgery to place pins and screws in his legs and ankle, but he would be able to play again after rehabilitation. He would miss the rest of the season, but the doctors expected a full recovery. I was relieved and happy for him. It was strange; even though our injuries were totally different, his good news gave me a little hope.

As I was called in to see the doctor, that hope quickly shifted to apprehension. As I entered the doctor's office, I could see pictures of my x-rays posted on the wall. I tried to make out something from the x-rays while waiting for the doctor, but I could not make sense of the images. Minutes stretched on like hours as I waited for the doctor. My wife and I had prayed that morning; I continued that same prayer while I waited and asked the Lord for His will, not mine, to be done. My main concern was that I could be out for the rest of the NFL Europe season, or possibly even into the upcoming season when I was slated to return back to the NFL in the United States. Finally, the doctor entered the room. I could tell from his expression that the news was grim. He spent a few minutes asking questions about my pain level and looking over my charts before speaking.

"Tyrone . . ." there was a slight hesitation. I felt my breath draw in as he continued. "The result of your x-ray shows a fracture to your T5 vertebra." The T5 vertebra is the fifth of the twelve thoracic vertebrae. It is located along the spinal column between the shoulders. He pointed to a place on the x-ray, and I could make out a small jagged line on the picture. My eyes shifted from doctor to x-ray and back to the doctor. "With this type of injury, if you were to continue playing football, it could result in permanent disability."

It took a moment for his words to register. *Permanent disability?* I could not possibly have heard him correctly. I sat in silence as I juggled the words in my brain. No matter what I did, I could not make sense of the doctor's words.

"I'm sorry, Doctor, but I don't understand." I met him eye to eye because I needed clarity and wanted no misunderstandings. "Do you mean if I continue playing this season? If I don't give the injuries time to heal?"

The doctor sighed and shook his head. His expression looked weary. "No, I am afraid this is a permanent recommendation that you do not continue playing football, or you risk serious injury to your neck and spinal cord." He confirmed my greatest fear. "Tyrone, the damage is significant enough that if you receive even one strong hit, you could lose the ability to walk."

I sat stunned, silent, emotionally paralyzed by the news. This could not be real. Not when my career was taking off and everything was going so well for me on the field. I swallowed hard and stared out the window at a passing car, trying to think of something to ask, some loophole he was not mentioning . . . a surgical procedure . . . anything. My mind was already moving toward getting a second and third opinion, but I knew that the doctor in front of me was one of the best in his field.

He spoke for a while longer, trying to address my unasked questions, but hardly anything registered with me. All I could hear was the thunderous pounding of my heart, racing toward the finish line of my career. I had not seen the end of my career in football as even a possibility at the beginning of the day. As a player, I was focused on maintaining my health and fitness. I did not drink or smoke; I did not go out and party. I was always a hard worker in practice and conscientious on the field in order to avoid injuries. I was supposed to play professional football for at least ten years. Even as I prayed and encouraged my teammate while we waited, I had assured him that his life was bigger than football. I had not imagined being the one who would receive a career-ending prognosis. I was not sure what my next step would be, but I knew one thing for certain—I was not going to give up without a good fight.

When my wife and I returned from Spain to the United States, we spent weeks seeing some of the NFL's best doctors. It was recommended that I spend eight months rehabilitating at a facility in Birmingham, Alabama. I met professional athletes from nearly every sport, from baseball to wrestling, all with the same goals of recuperating from their injuries and getting back to the sport that they loved.

> *"Let me tell you the secret that has led me to my goal. My strength lies solely in my tenacity."*
>
> *- Louis Pasteur*

Many of the athletes had been given the equivalent of career death sentences, but they refused to give up. I knew the likelihood of playing again with my type of injury was slim. For a defensive player, a fracture to the vertebra was disastrous. There was too great a chance that the injury could reoccur, and very few teams would take the chance; still, it was worth it to try. I held on to the hope that my rehabilitation would be successful and a team would still want me to play for them.

Every day I followed the same routine. I would rehabilitate my back for three hours in the morning, eat and rest a few hours in my hotel room, and then I would return for another three hours of rehabilitation. It was a monotonous and arduous schedule, and with my wife living in Houston, I spent the majority of my time alone reflecting on my injury and how it would affect the rest of my life. During this time, it hit me that there was a possibility that my football career was over. I spent days feeling angry, frustrated, and sorry for myself. It wasn't long before I began to realize that feeling this way was not going to heal my back or feed my family. Many of the other injured athletes at the facility relied solely on their sport and had nothing to fall back on. Some had not finished college and were devastated that their dreams could be ending.

Knowing that I had a degree that I had worked so hard to earn kept me from feeling like I had failed. I remembered a Bible study I attended while in training camp with the Washington Redskins a year prior to my injury. It was led by one of the NFL's greatest cornerbacks, Darrell Green, who played for nearly 20 years with the Washington Redskins. He had always been one of my greatest inspirations because of his work on the field, and because he was a man of integrity *off the field*. A large number of players attended the Bible study each day after training camp practice. I remember Darrell Green looking intently at each of us, and expressing that every man has a defined purpose in his life. Then he asked if we knew our true purpose in life. Everyone in the room was silent. My thoughts immediately went to the game of football as a part of my purpose.

It was the game that I lived and breathed. . . yes, of course it was my purpose. He told us to think about when we were in elementary school and went on a field trip. The field trip was the highlight of the year for many of us. We had a lot of fun and wanted to stay on the field trip forever. That was not reality. At the end of the day, once the field trip was over, we still had to get on the bus and go back to school.

"The NFL is like going on a field trip," Darrell Green told us. "Eventually, you have to continue with your life after your time in the NFL comes to an end. Your life, your purpose, is much bigger than your career as a professional football player." He would even joke that NFL stands for "Not for Long." What he said resonated with me, and I held on to those words, repeating them to myself after my injury. During my rehabilitation, I often thought back to Darrell asking us, "What is your true passion in life? What do you love so much that you would do it without pay? Find that, and you may have found your true purpose."

After spending eight months rehabilitating my back, I went back to the doctors hoping to be cleared to play. Everywhere I went, the news was the same. I could continue to play, but I ran a very high risk of incurring a debilitating injury. This was not good news for me, or any football organization interested in signing me. It came down to answering this question: Was risking my ability to walk worth continuing to play the game that I loved, the game that I had worked so hard at for so many years?

It was one of the most difficult decisions that I would ever make. I remembered that I had prayed for the Lord's will in my life, and I knew that His will for me was to no longer be on the football field. As hard as it was to make the decision to walk away, I had to do just that in order to make sure that I could continue to walk in the future.

For so long, football had been the driving force in my life. All of my decisions and choices had been centered on the game and on building a career from it. I had not been naïve enough to think that I would play football forever, but I had hoped for a long career. Now I was forced to consider other options. As I pondered my choices, I thought back to my childhood and the journey that led to the decision that would shape my life.

I was a young, black man. I was not supposed to have dreams outside of the streets that I grew up on. I was not afraid of failure. After all, failure seemed inevitable when you grow up in a world where you are not expected to live to see the age of 25, at least not without a criminal record. Life back then was supposed to teach me that hope was a waste. Life was designed to help me understand very early that my choices were limited to being a criminal or a victim, a dealer or an addict, the predator or the prey. Even if I recognized the fact that I had some skill or talent, some potential for greatness, or a desire to be exceptional, I had a keen sense that the choices and failures from the neighborhood were still waiting for me.

I knew it was all right to fail. I knew it was expected of me. So I was not afraid of failure; I was terrified of it. Even greater than my terror was my pure, blinding hatred at the very thought that failure could control my life. Every day I was haunted by the vision of what I would become if I failed. I saw that image every day in Third Ward. As I walked the streets of my neighborhood, I saw person after person living with the consequences of bad choices. In them, I would see glimpses of the defeated man I could so easily become. Looking into their empty and soulless eyes, devoid of compassion, I saw that they were beyond the point of redemption, with hearts full of bitterness and regret. I knew that it would kill me if I ever allowed myself to forget what the alternative to success looked like. I could not allow myself to fail.

As I pondered over my post-injury decision, I thought back over my childhood and the things that inspired me. I remembered that as a child, my parents were always helping our neighbors, feeding the homeless, and trying to make our community a better place. Watching them make a difference in the lives of others created a desire in me to do the same, and it prompted me to choose sociology as my major in college.

During the off-season of my rookie year with the San Francisco 49ers, I trained at a high school in Houston with my mentor, Dennis Brantley. It was in that environment that I first felt a strong desire to work with youth. One day I noticed a group of students who had decided to skip school in the middle of the day. I watched as the students were leaving campus and trying to avoid getting caught. Part of me wanted to stop them and ask them where they were headed and what was more important than getting their education. I wondered if the kids had anyone at home pushing them to succeed. Maybe they had never learned to value the opportunities they could receive through education. I remembered how it felt to grow up with so many negative influences on every corner, and how important it was to have someone care enough to want to see me make good choices.

I never forgot that day. I realized then that I had a powerful urge to reach out to kids with backgrounds similar to my own and to help them learn how to succeed. At the time, I did not even know where or how I would start trying to impact the lives of kids in that way. Once I returned home after my injury, it started to become clear. I was asked to speak at a school assembly, and I took the opportunity to reach out and engage the youth in honest conversations about their futures. I talked to them on their level.

I shared my story, and many of the students approached me afterwards to tell me that it was the first time they felt inspired to make positive changes in their lives. They expressed interest in goals, such as attending college and finding their life's purpose. I saw a real need for programs that would not only keep the students motivated, but also teach them the necessary tools to reach their dreams. Soon after this experience, I began First and Goal, Inc. At the time, I did not know that this would become my purpose, but now I feel that nothing I ever accomplished on the football field could compare to the impact First and Goal has made in the lives of the thousands of youth and young adults that we have reached through our programs since 1999.

First and Goal, Inc. is a 501c(3) non-profit whose mission is to provide the necessary tools, support, and resources for youth that will enrich, equip, and empower them to become effective members of society. It is through the organization's slogan, *"A Game Plan for Life"*, that youth are encouraged to become active participants in achieving their dreams. Academic failure, lack of positive role models, negative peer pressure, low self-esteem, poor social skills, youth violence, and a lack of leadership and coping skills are a few of the issues that create obstacles for youth in reaching their potential and fulfilling their dreams. First and Goal, Inc. has effectively developed programs that attend to the sensitive issues facing today's youth by implementing a consistent, personalized approach. In the world of athletics, it has often been said that, "It's not whether you win or lose, but how you play the game." This slogan is used to encourage our youth to develop their unique *"Game Plan for Life"*, and First and Goal, Inc. is fully committed and dedicated in its efforts to provide programs that make this concept come to life in each of its program participants. First and Goal, Inc. has had the privilege of positively influencing thousands of youth across the United States.

Life outside of the game of football has allowed me to recognize that my desire to make a great impact in the lives of others is my purpose. Your experiences in life will lead you to your purpose as well. Once you identify your purpose in life, it is important that you follow through on your intense desire to fulfill this purpose, no matter what it takes. You may sometimes discover your purpose in the most unexpected way, and if you remain enthusiastic, your path will soon become clear.

Each of us has a calling or a purpose. It is something that we love doing and that we know how to do so well that we deeply desire to share it with the world. It is like a dream, but more than a dream; it is your dearest dream. However, your dream can only become a reality if you truly believe in it. You see, in order for your dreams to come into existence, you must feed them with your own beliefs. You are capable of achieving greatness in life, but you have to believe it. Listen to your heart. Follow your dreams. Find your purpose.

. . . . . ● ● . . . .

KEY POINT:

- ◆ Identify your purpose and develop goals to fulfill your purpose.

KEY ACTION:

- ◆ All of us have a defined purpose in life. Will you choose to believe that you are destined for greatness?

"You see, we feed our dreams with our own beliefs. Will you feed your dreams so that they will grow healthy and strong, or will you let them starve?"

- Tyrone Smith: Outside the Huddle

OUTSIDE
the
HUDDLE

OUTSIDE

the

HUDDLE

Steps to Developing a Game Plan for Life

PITFALLS

. . . . . ● . . . . .

"Wanting something is not enough. You must hunger for it. Your motivation must be absolutely compelling in order to overcome the obstacles that will invariably come your way."

-Les Brown

When I began to understand the true purpose of my life, I felt as if I had found a light to guide me out of a darkness that I did not realize I was stumbling through. But it was not long before the shadows began to move back into my path. Whether these shadows came in the form of friends, family, colleagues, or myself, I began to deal with opposition and negativity almost immediately. What I have learned throughout my experiences is that pitfalls, obstacles, and failures are inevitable, but they do not have to stop your show. When you recognize these experiences as life lessons, you can conquer them and use them as motivators toward success.

Throughout my life others have tried to measure me by my successes and accomplishments. They failed to realize that I have had just as many, if not more, failures in my life. One of the biggest mistakes that people make in life is not embracing the fact that failures, obstacles, and pitfalls help to shape you. As you set out to meet certain goals, dreams, hopes, and aspirations, know that along the way there will be trials. When faced with these obstacles, will you allow them to get the better of you, or will you instead overcome them to accomplish your goals?

One my greatest pitfalls in my life came when I was fourteen years old and in the eighth grade my parents got divorced. I arrived home from school one day after football practice, and I was not expecting the news. I was in a very good mood because I had an awesome football practice, and I was excited about the upcoming game. All the way home from practice, I thought about the delicious homemade hamburgers that my mother would cook for dinner every Wednesday night, but to my surprise, she was not at home. I knew that something was wrong because my mother knew that I looked forward to Wednesday nights because of those burgers. I knocked on my dad's bedroom door and asked where my mom was, and he responded, "She is not here, and I will talk to you later, Tyrone." My dad was in his room with the door locked, and it was obvious that he had a lot on his mind. I could hear it in his voice. The household was silent; my brothers, my cousin, and my half-sister were all quiet. I wanted to know what was going on. I later found out that my mother had left.

I was in a bad place—a sad place—where I was frustrated all of the time. How could this happen to me? My family structure was broken, and I felt it in my heart every day. My parents did not even offer an explanation for the break-up. I did not know how to cope with my feelings, and I simply gave up. I did not care about school; I did not care about my health; I did not care about anything. I was bitter and angry, and I did not know how to deal with the pain that I was feeling. My way of coping with the pain and the loss was by being the best boxer that I could be. Yes, the best boxer! What I mean is that I started fighting all of the time. I didn't know what else to do to cope with it and I needed a place to channel all of that frustration. So, I would fight with students at my school for the simplest reasons. It was my outlet for dealing with the ongoing pain and loss. If you touched me on my head, I would fight. If you talked about the way that I looked, I would fight. If you talked about my shoes, I would fight. If you talked about me playing football on the "B" team, I would fight. If you talked negatively about anything, I would fight. I was constantly looking for a reason to unleash my anger.

I soon found out that I could not continue to deal with my pain in this way. I had to stop fighting. You can only hit people and run so many times before they catch you and retaliate. Fighting had become too brutal. I knew that I needed to find another way of coping with the pain of my parents' divorce. My time as a boxer was up, and I stopped fighting.

After I realized that fighting was not the best way to cope with my hurt, I started coping with the pain in a different way. I refused to take a bath. Emotionally, I was trying to find a way to deal with the great loss and pain that still troubled me. I figured that this behavior would show my parents how their personal issues had affected me. Maybe they would notice that I did not bathe and ask me what was going on. I was not a talkative kid; I was not expressive with my parents, so this was the way I chose to get their attention. Once they realized that I was crying out, maybe they would get back together, or so I hoped.

Not bathing each day was a very unhealthy way to deal with my emotions, but what else could I do? I would walk down the hallway at school, and my friends would say, "Somebody smells really bad!" I would agree and start to look around in order to take the attention off myself. For almost a month, I did not bathe or brush my teeth. I did not care about going to school. I did not care about how I looked. I did not even care about how I smelled. I did not know how to deal with my emotions concerning the divorce in a healthy way.

One hot and humid Houston morning during my personal bathing strike, I missed the school bus and had to walk three miles to school. This magnified my frustration. While walking to school I began to sweat a lot, and I could really smell myself. It was terrible, as you can imagine. The heat, exhaustion, and smell added to my frustration. I finally arrived at school, relieved to feel the cool air conditioning. At that moment I knew that I wasn't hurting anyone but myself. I also realized I had no control over the decision my mom and dad made to get a divorce, but I did have control over my own actions and behavior. In life we will experience obstacles, circumstances, and situations that we have no control over, but from those experiences we can become stronger. I had to come to this realization in order to gain control of my life.

Focus on recognizing, conquering, and overcoming pitfalls and obstacles; using failed experiences as motivation can move you toward success.

- Tyrone Smith

· · · · ● ● · · · ·

I now know that you must remain prepared for the battles that unexpectedly arise in your life. Only when you are unprepared do you lose the fight, just as I had done when my parents divorced. I would eventually find myself unprepared once again.

During my freshman year at Baylor University, I was considered a redshirt freshman on the football team. This meant that I would not play during my freshman year, but I would still fulfill my academic requirements and attend classes. This would allow me an additional year of playing eligibility after completing my degree in four years. This put me in the perfect position during my senior year, because I had already earned my degree and achieved my goal of graduating from college. I was now able to work toward my Master's Degree, but I could also place greater focus on the game of football and my plan to play in the National Football League. NFL scouts began visiting me during my junior year, and I was already projected to be a late-round NFL draft pick. I was one of the top cornerbacks in the Southwest Conference, which is now a part of the Big 12 Conference. It was the year that I thought nothing could go wrong, until everything went wrong in a single moment.

> *"Obstacles don't have to stop you. If you run into a wall, don't turn around and give up. Figure out how to climb it, go through it, or work around it."*
>
> *- Michael Jordan*

We were playing our fifth game of the season against the University of Houston at the Astrodome. It was a huge game for me because I was playing in my hometown in front of my friends and family. I always had extremely good games against the University of Houston because of the excitement from being back at home. The University of Houston players were talking trash and trying to get me off of my game, but they had no idea that I was on a mission to crush them. During the game one of the wide receivers attempted to "cut block" me, a potentially dangerous maneuver of trying to make a block by diving at the feet or ankles of the defensive player (in this instance, me). I grabbed the wide receiver and threw him to the ground. As he fell he grabbed my jersey, taking me down with him. My foot had gotten caught in the turf, and an excruciating pain rushed through my ankle. Immediately, I knew something was seriously wrong. I could not move my ankle, and I had to be helped off of the field.

That night I remained with my family in Houston. My ankle had already swollen to two times its normal size, and I knew that the injury was severe. I couldn't stop myself from thinking of the worst-case scenario. I was afraid this might be the end of football for me, and I had expected so much out of my last year. I knew that having an injury my last season in college would greatly affect my chances of making it to the NFL. My brother Harold tried to make light of the situation by telling me that I was trying to do too much during the game by going after the wide receiver. His comments only increased my feelings of frustration. Harold's comments affected me. Despite the fact that he had just been released from prison, I expected more encouragement from him at the time. How could he even understand what I was experiencing? He had not played college football and was not preparing to play on the next level in the NFL. At the time, I felt that he was being a hater, or a negative influence, because of his own unfulfilled dreams. My fiancée, DeMonica, tried to encourage me, but I could not hear her through my frustration. It felt as if I was the only one who realized that this could be my undoing. All that I could think about was my dream of playing in the NFL not becoming a reality.

The next day I returned to Baylor University in Waco, Texas. I went to the doctor to find out that I had slightly torn three ligaments in my ankle and could possibly miss the rest of the season. I was devastated by the news. This was supposed to be the greatest season of my college career. This was the season when I wanted to show NFL scouts exactly what *Tyrone Smith* could do for their teams. Now I knew that would be impossible. I felt helpless. All that I could do was work hard on rehabilitating my ankle, and hope to play again before the season ended.

It is very hard to describe what a physical injury does mentally to an athlete. No matter how hard you work to remain positive, eventually the limitations that injuries place on your body can wear you down and make you feel like a failure. I had never felt so defeated. Worst of all, I felt that no one understood what I was going through. My fiancée was living in Houston, and although her frequent calls to check on me always lifted my spirits, it was not the same as having DeMonica physically present.

I began to withdraw from everyone and to go inside myself. I stopped talking to my friends as often as I used to because I did not want to answer their questions about how I was doing. My family expected me to become a big football sensation, and I now felt that it was no longer possible. I felt that I had let everyone down, including myself.

My lowest point came after a visit from an NFL scout for the Miami Dolphins. My ankle still required a lot of rehabilitation before I could walk without limping. The Dolphins' scout even knew my name. I was surprised to hear that he was visiting Baylor University for the sole purpose of watching me practice. The scout kept asking me if I could do any drills whatsoever, even just run a straight line so that he would have something to report to the team about me. At that point, I could barely walk, let alone run. It was extremely disheartening to see how disappointed the scout was because he would have nothing to report about my progress. Prior to my injury I was projected to be a late round draft pick for the NFL. At that moment, I could feel the hope of that dream draining away.

I soon decided to take action. Every night DeMonica and I would pray together over the phone, and I began to realize that I needed a support system in Waco to help me get through this time. I joined Nexus Bible Study group, a campus Bible study and student support group at Baylor University. The group helped me take my focus off of my injury and put it back on God. It was at this time that I realized my life was bigger than the game of football.

In my private time, I prayed, and I could feel God comforting me and letting me know that even in my darkest time He was holding me close. I found peace once I discovered this, and my faith was renewed. I did not ask God to allow me to continue playing football. He already knew that the desire of my heart was to finish the season with my teammates and to continue playing the game that I loved. I asked that He would restore me physically, mentally, and spiritually to allow me to do His will.

It took weeks of work and rehabilitation, but finally my ankle was sufficiently healed to allow me to play the last three games of the season with my team. I was able to finish strong and celebrate my accomplishments while still being a part of the Baylor Bears.

> *"The road to success is always under construction."*
>
> *- Lily Tomlin*

Shortly after the season ended, I started to prepare for the NFL draft, hoping that my dream of playing in the National Football League would come true. I had accomplished and overcome a lot in my life, and I felt that it would be the ultimate achievement to make it to the next level. The NFL draft came and went in April of 1996. I was not drafted, but the San Francisco 49ers contacted me shortly after. The success of my college career had earned me an opportunity to participate in the San Francisco 49ers minicamp following the draft for rookies and veterans. I earned a place on the team as an undrafted free agent. The dream that I thought would never come to fruition finally became a reality. From this experience I learned the greatest lesson: never give up on yourself, no matter what obstacles seem to lie ahead. Even the smallest chance of achieving success is worth grasping and holding on to with every fiber of your being.

In life we are all going to have failed experiences or pitfalls. The question is: when you have these experiences, how will you respond? Will you respond in a way that makes you feel empowered because you have learned something from the experience? Will you use the life lesson to build your character as a survivor? From failed experiences in life, you learn the following:

- How to take a self-inventory. You learn what not to do by understanding what works best for you.
- How to do things better. You begin to think and perform more effectively.
- Failed experiences make you stronger in order to prepare for other challenges in life. The key is how you respond to the failure. Failure can be a character builder that empowers you for the journey of life.

On your path to glory, you will run into unexpected pitfalls. Not everything will be pleasant on your journey in life. Sometimes you will fail. You will fall. You will want to run away and give up so avidly that you may start doubting your dream altogether. But, whenever you run into that obstacle or fail miserably, instead of giving up on your dreams, look at it as a temporary roadblock. No matter how difficult it seems to be, there is always a way; there is always a solution; and there is always a way out. Sometimes the bigger the obstacle or harder you fall, the stronger you will rise. Know that obstacles and failures have lessons for you to learn about yourself, others, the world, and life. Just receive what you are meant to learn and know that it will help you on your journey. Pitfalls should be used to teach you how to be flexible, how to adapt, how to crawl, and how to soar. It is all a part of your journey.

. . . . . ● . . . . .

KEY POINT:

◆ Life is a journey and not a destination. Along the way you will experience pitfalls, but you must remain focused on your goals.

KEY ACTION:

◆ Recognize the pitfalls and understand that obstacles will always be present, but know that you can overcome any opposition.

> *"Anything that I see as a challenge in life is just a mountain before me, and I believe that I can move and conquer the mountain."*
>
> *- Antonio Armstrong*

"In life we will experience obstacles, circum-stances, and situations that we have no control over, but through it all we will become stronger."

- *Tyrone Smith: Outside the Huddle*

OUTSIDE *the* HUDDLE

Steps to Developing a Game Plan for Life

OUTSIDE *the* HUDDLE

Steps to Developing a Game Plan for Life

PEOLE

. . . .

"There are two types of people—achievers and doubters."

-Tyrone Smith

Everyone is capable of achieving success. Whether or not you succeed is determined by your belief in yourself. There are many different types of people in this world, but it's extremely important for you to know what type of person you are. Your success and how you go about achieving success depends on it. This section focuses on two types of people—achievers and doubters. You will learn how to identify and choose which type of person you are, and learn the importance of surrounding yourself with the right type of people to achieve your goals.

Are you an achiever or a doubter? This is an important question to ask yourself before approaching any task. An achiever is someone who works diligently to accomplish goals and keeps at a task until progress is made. Achievers recognize that accomplishing anything in life comes with a price that may include failures and discomforts, but they are willing to make their dreams happen in spite of their struggles. On the other hand, a doubter is someone who does not believe. At first they may believe in trying to accomplish something, but they easily give up when encountering hardships or failures, convinced that a particular goal is not attainable. A doubter has no true drive, no true desire, and no true belief in himself/herself.

I wonder how much more effective a doubter's life would be if they were willing to surround themselves with the right people. We truly can never accomplish anything without supportive people in our lives. I am thankful for the people who have supported and encouraged me along my journey. I know I have not accomplished anything by myself; it took the support of those around me to help me reach my goals. People often look at successful professional athletes as heroes, but they are simply individuals who have chosen to surround themselves with supportive, uplifting, and positive people—achievers. Every athlete has a story to tell about the people who have helped him or her along the way. So, again I ask you, which type of person are you?

Even if you have just realized that you are a doubter, it is important to know that it is possible to become an achiever. It is also important to know that it will take hard work and there may be unexpected results and trials along the way, but true achievers are able to remain motivated despite adversity. My father always said, "A quitter never wins, and a winner never quits."

My dad knew a little something about quitters and winners from his personal experiences. He had his own dreams of playing professional football—in fact, it was all that he focused on when he was growing up. Playing professional football was his number one goal in life. When he was in high school in Jasper, Texas, he injured his knee in a football game. After the knee injury in the eleventh grade, he decided that there was no value in continuing his education because he would not be able to play football. He had put all of his hope and trust into the game of football, and suddenly his hopes and dreams were crushed. He quit school and never returned. He would often have trouble finding a good job because he did not complete high school. He eventually turned to the truck driving industry because he couldn't find any other form of gainful employment. Years later, my dad would often tell me how he truly regretted dropping out of school. As he got older, he realized that the lack of an education made things harder for him. Since my father struggled early in life because of his decision to drop out of school, he encouraged my brothers and me to value our education. He was very strict when it came to education because he knew that if we applied ourselves academically, life would be so much better for us. Even though he realized years ago that quitting school was a mistake, he still lives with that regret today. My father's story presents a simple, but powerful message that achievers like myself know to be true: "Don't quit."

I learned not to quit early in life. When I was ten years old, my parents decided to move our family out of the inner city of Houston to a new home in the suburbs. It was a major sacrifice for us to move from our neighborhood in Third Ward to Missouri City, Texas, just outside of Houston. Both of my parents took on additional jobs working long hours to fund our move, but because Missouri City was an area with less crime and violence and better schools, my parents knew their sacrifices would be worth it. My brothers and I were not too thrilled to move away from our friends, but we loved our new, bigger and nicer home. I especially loved the backyard, where I would spend hours playing games or hanging out by myself. I was so thankful just to have a yard with grass.

The first day at my new school, Ridgemont Elementary, I was extremely nervous. I never realized, until now, how much my first week at this new school would impact the rest of my life. When I walked into the classroom, I felt that every eye was on me. My teacher made me stand in front of the class to introduce myself. I was very shy and quiet at that age and dreaded speaking in front of people. I was so scared that I could barely speak, but I managed to mumble quick answers to my teacher's questions.

When she asked me where I had moved from and I told her Third Ward, I heard low murmurs throughout the classroom. Third Ward had a reputation for being a rough neighborhood. I could tell some of the kids immediately labeled me as a troubled kid because I was from there. Even my teacher misinterpreted my shyness and thought I was purposely being difficult. It did not help that a few days before starting at my new school I accidentally cut my wrist with a sharp knife while washing dishes. When my teacher noticed my bandaged wrist and asked me what had happened, I responded by mumbling, "I got cut with a knife." After that, she quickly had me take my seat. The other students were whispering around me, and I heard the words "knife fight." I felt a warm flush sweep over my face. I knew that I had made a bad first impression.

At lunch, the other students avoided me. Every now and then, someone would look at me and quickly turn away, but no one would sit by me or talk to me. I spent most of my lunch staring miserably at my food and wondering what my friends were doing at my old school without me.

I wanted to find a hole to crawl in to get away from the

stares, the pointing, and the whispers. More than anything, I wanted to be back at my old school with all of the kids that I had grown up with. I did not want to be the new kid that everyone was trying to figure out. It seemed that most of the kids thought that they had already figured me out and had determined that I was not worth getting to know. It felt so unfair to not be given a chance. During recess, I leaned against an abandoned tetherball pole while I watched the other kids play. Out of nowhere, someone pushed me from behind, and I went sprawling into the dirt. I looked up to see three boys standing over me, sneering. I clenched my hands into fists, my palms burning from the impact with the ground.

"Who pushed me?" I asked. My eyes were already watering from my anger. The bullies ignored my question, laughing at me as I quickly rose to my feet. I saw a crowd beginning to form around us.

"You need to go back to where you came from," one of the boys shouted. "We don't need ghetto trash around here!" I could not believe what I was hearing. No one had ever called me anything like that or picked a fight with me. The misery of the day was pressing against me, culminating in this one event. My heart was thundering in my chest.

"You don't even know me," I said, stepping closer to the boy who had spoken. I figured he was also the one who had pushed me to the ground. "You better get out of my face!" I snarled at the boy who pushed me down. The crowd began to chant "Fight! Fight!" and, before I realized what was happening, I found myself rolling around on the ground with the bully, kicking and punching for all I was worth. Soon, the playground attendant pulled us off of one another and sent us to the principal's office.

"I don't know about your previous school, but this type of behavior will not be tolerated here, Mr. Smith," the principal said to me. At my old school, I never got into trouble, but I was already being labeled as a troublemaker on my first day at a new school. No one would listen to my side of the story, and I felt that it was because I was a kid from the inner city.

To make matters worse, I was placed in a regular level class and I struggled from day one. Here I was in the fourth grade; the teacher had given various math problems for the class to solve, and I was totally clueless. I didn't understand the information that she was covering; she may as well have been speaking in a foreign language. I later found out that she was reviewing multiplication and preparing the class for division. I struggled for the first two weeks of school before they moved me to a lower level class. I already had low self-confidence, and this was another transition that I had to deal with in the short amount of time at my new school. My new fourth grade teacher was not engaging, and I felt that I was less than the average fourth grader. She failed to connect with me as a student and as an individual.

Weeks went by without me making any friends. I felt sick to my stomach every morning at the thought of returning to school. It seemed like every day, different kids wanted to prove how tough they were by taking on the kid from Third Ward. I had always been a good student, but my grades began to drop because I could not concentrate on schoolwork. My parents were not involved because they were working a lot, trying to establish themselves in a new community. For me, it all seemed to be too much. Living in a new community and trying to adjust to a new school proved to be overwhelming; I did not know how to process my emotions. I did not even tell my older brothers. I internalized it all, which, in retrospect, was not the healthiest way to deal with everything. All that I wanted was a supportive teacher who could offer hope, guidance, and direction; I was not receiving that from this teacher.

My teacher barely spoke to me unless it was for a disciplinary reason. It seemed as if she had formed an opinion of me along with everyone else. I began to hate school, and I slowly was becoming a different person. Before, I had been shy and introverted, but still a good student. Now, I felt hopeless and confused about the things that were happening to me. As a result, I decided that if everyone treated me like a thug, then that's who I would be. I began to talk back to the teacher during class and get into fights with the other students. During the fourth grade, I was sent to the principal's office more than fifty times for various disciplinary issues. The worst part was that I knew I was going in the wrong direction, but I no longer cared; I was so hurt and angry by the way people treated me that I let it dictate my actions. When the school year ended I was relieved and happy because I could forget about the school, the teacher, and the kids—at least for the summer. By the time I began fifth grade, I already had earned a reputation for being a troublemaker. I figured that fifth grade would be more of the same. I would constantly get into fights and be sent to the principal's office like before, but I was completely wrong. Things were about to change.

My fifth-grade teacher, Mrs. Williams, became my saving grace. After my first fight as one of her students, Mrs. Williams sat me down after school. She asked me why I felt the need to prove myself by fighting. Initially, I shrugged and told her that I did not know. As we talked more, I finally was able to open up. I told her that I never wanted to fight and that I had actually been a good student at my previous school.

"Tyrone, you are so very special," she said to me. "You are a smart boy, and you are capable of doing great things in your life. But you can't let people get in your way. I have seen so many of my students never reach their potential for that very reason. I want you to prove to me and everyone else that you are better than that."

She hugged me, and I turned away, trying not to let her see the tears in my eyes. For the first time since I had started attending Ridgemont Elementary, I felt that someone cared enough to listen to me and to see the *real* me. After that day, I would talk to Mrs. Williams whenever I felt angry or frustrated, and she would help me resolve my problems without fighting or acting out. Mrs. Williams did not speak to me like most adult authority figures spoke to kids. She took the time to listen to my concerns and to reach me on my level. It was through these interactions that I learned not to be reactive. I learned that I did not have to debate every opinion and that sometimes I would gain more from listening to others than from trying to be right. It was Mrs. Williams who showed me that sometimes what a child needs most is to be heard and to be treated like they matter. It is a lesson that I have carried with me into adulthood and into my work with youth.

My grades improved dramatically, and I was never sent to the principal's office during the fifth grade. The only call my mother received from the principal that year was to ask her to keep me home longer in the mornings because I was arriving at school before the staff. I loved being at school again, and I started making friends. I even began to overcome my shyness and let people see the real me. Mrs. Williams helped me rebuild my sense of self-worth and made me realize that it does not matter what people say I am; what matters is who

I know I am. I have always remembered what she taught me about myself and how to deal with others.

> *"Facing pitfalls throughout my life has often caused me to ask two essential questions: What type of person do I want to be, and what type of people do I want to surround myself with in order to reach my goals?"*
>
> *- Tyrone Smith*

Another person who helped me through this transitional time was my best friend in fifth grade, Roderick McKenzie. Roderick was one of the most popular kids in the school. His presence was always positive, despite the fact that others treated me unfairly. He saw me acting out and came alongside to support and encourage me. It was truly a good thing to have a friend to talk to during the times when I felt bad about my situation. His friendship proved peer-to-peer influence can be life-changing; everyone, regardless of age, has the opportunity to make an impact in the life of another person. I can truly say that Roderick McKenzie is my best friend.

Friends are people who trust each other because of their special, shared bond. Having a true friend is important because you have a person that you can connect with to share feelings and struggles. A true friend is supportive, not judgmental, and trustworthy in all situations—the individual that genuinely cares about your well-being through difficult situations in life. Overall, to have someone there in moments of need is key to your personal growth, as you learn from and share knowledge with others. In life we go through experiences that make us stronger, and having a person to support you through those times is critical.

My elementary school experiences with the people who doubted me prepared me for the various challenges in life that I would later face. The doubters inspired me to become a better, more caring person toward those in need because I was once that person in need. Even though I didn't think so at the time, having doubters in my life during my early childhood taught me the greatest lesson I could have learned—to believe in myself and to genuinely care for others. I learned to achieve.

· · · · ● · · · · ·

In life there will be people who will disappoint you. The disappointments may cause you pain and confusion, but the key to overcoming those disappointments is discovering how you can grow from the experience. It is up to you to realize that you can learn from all situations in life, both good and bad.

Growing up, I loved the game of football. Playing football in my new neighborhood made me feel free. It was my greatest outlet to express my energy, passion, and competitive edge. It was a joy to have such a great love for the game, and I enjoyed watching football at any level, from the local little league games to professional football. As a kid, I would watch a football game, and then go outside to mimic the moves that I had just seen on television; it was so inspiring to me. My oldest brother, Harold Jr., played high school football with a guy that would one day become a superstar in college and in the National Football League. I watched these guys play on Friday nights at the local district football stadium, and I could not wait for my opportunity to wear the same uniform and play on the same football field.

The superstar that I mentioned had a phenomenal senior year playing football, and every college in the nation recruited him. This running back had a tremendous amount of talent and skill, and everyone loved to watch him run the football. After he had signed his letter of intent to go to college, my brother Harold came home one day and told me that he had a surprise for me.

I was shocked that he had a surprise for me; this wasn't something he would normally do. I was curious to know what the surprise was and excited to hear what he had to say. Harold told me that he told the local football star how much I loved football and asked him if he would be willing to visit me. My brother went on to tell me that the football star lived only five minutes away and had agreed to stop by our house to visit me the following Saturday. I was so excited because I was going to meet a true football superstar in person, and I was ecstatic that he was willing to take the time from his busy schedule to visit me. I was ready to hear whatever he had to share.

I had just finished playing my little league football season a few weeks earlier, so this experience would be the culminating event of an awesome football season. I was so excited the Friday night before my anticipated visit with the superstar that I could hardly sleep. When Saturday morning came, I could not hide my excitement. I put on my number twenty-eight Redskins jersey and matching maroon shorts. I hurried to wash my face, brush my teeth, and eat my morning bowl of Frosted Flakes cereal. After breakfast I waited with a smile on my face, constantly asking Harold, Jr. when the superstar was coming. His response was always the same: "Patience, Tyrone."

Lunchtime rolled around, and I was still excited about the opportunity to meet the soon-to-be-football-legend. I still had that smile on my face, constantly asking my brother when the superstar was coming, and his response was still the same: "Patience, Tyrone . . . patience." I waited and waited and waited, but he never showed up. As the darkness of the night dimmed the front porch where I sat in front of our house, heaviness filled my heart. I was hurt, mad, frustrated, and confused. How could he make a commitment and not keep it? He had an opportunity to use his influence to encourage a young life, and he chose not to. That moment of disappointment made me realize that at times in life, people will fail you. It took me some time to realize that these disappointments should not be taken personally. When others fail you in life, it is a reflection of their character, and not yours. Know that people will fail you at times, but do not let this discourage you from using those disappointments to become a better person to others.

It is critical that you are true to yourself and that you are a person of integrity when you commit yourself to something, even if that something is as simple as paying a visit to someone. Our influence can be used to make a great difference in the world, but only if we use it in the right way. I did not know at the time how instrumental that experience would be in building one of my key principles regarding using my influence to impact the lives of others. I have made a commitment to be a man of my word and to show up and be present when I commit to doing something. I could have easily become a doubter back then, but that disappointment was not worth risking my will to achieve.

> "*Everyone is capable of achieving success. Whether you truly believe you can succeed makes the difference between those who do and those who do not.*"
>
> *-Tyrone Smith*

· · · · ● ✱ · · · ·

If you think about the different people who have impacted your life in a positive manner, a part of them is now a part of you. You know what it means to truly appreciate people for their heart as they give their time and support you in whatever you desire to do in life. I personally know what it means to be an achiever, and while I have experienced various hardships I still have the desire to overcome any situation and to persevere because of the people that I have encountered. I have been able to embody the mindset of an achiever because I have surrounded myself with achievers who have inspired me to become who I am today. I owe my gratitude to so many people.

Once I entered high school, my middle school coach, Dennis Brantley, took me aside and spoke the following truth to me: "Tyrone, you have no control over the situations in your life, but you do have control over YOUR life."

That simple statement was instrumental in re-directing my life toward a more positive path. He not only coached me on the field, but he coached me in life. He made a tremendous impact on me. Not only was he my mentor, but he was also a true example of a man that loved his family and one who worked to get the most out of all of his students. Coach Brantley was one of my football and track coaches, and he also taught history. He would always challenge me to do my best on the track and on the football field; but more importantly, he challenged me to do even better in the classroom. He saw something in me that I had not seen in myself. Even as a middle school student, I told myself that I would pattern my life after the way Coach Brantley lived his life. He lived and still lives his life with purpose, honor, and humility.

In the tenth grade, I found another source of inspiration in Ms. Burnett, my biology teacher. She left a lasting impression by teaching me to value my education and by inspiring me to learn more about science. Her passion for teaching and the joy she displayed were truly amazing and powerful. Even though I was not a science fan, she taught it in such a way that it became fascinating. Her style of teaching opened up my mind even more to embrace learning, which gave me a stronger sense of worth and value. Overall, Ms. Burnett created a classroom environment that helped me learn how to believe in myself. I hung on to her every word and earned all A's in her class. I learned that I could succeed academically when I applied myself.

The same year that I was impacted so greatly by Ms. Burnett, another influential person came into my life: Ms. Patricia Landheart. Ms. Landheart came into my life at a crucial time because I wasn't sure of what would happen next for me in my life. My dad had lost his job, his car, and subsequently our home. Losing our home was traumatic for me, and I was in constant fear of losing more. It was only two years after my parents' divorce, and to suffer another loss was truly devastating. I was embarrassed that we did not have a home to live in, and I did not want anyone to know about the issues that I was experiencing.

In order to compensate for not having a home, I would often hang out at different friends' homes longer than expected, waiting for dinnertime. The home where I stayed most was Cleveland Landheart's, aka Smokey; he was one of my teammates from the tenth grade football team. I would hang out at Smokey's house so often that his mother, Ms. Patricia Landheart, offered to take me in. I remember the day that my father came to pick me up from her home in a car that he borrowed from a friend. Ms. Landheart went out to speak with my father and let him know that it was all right for me to stay with her family full time. My father agreed and felt that it was the best thing for me at the time, but I knew it was hard for him. Ms. Landheart truly sacrificed for me and never asked my father for anything while I stayed at her home. She showed me love and support during that time and treated me like one of her own children. Their family, Ms. Landheart, Smokey, Marcus, and Daniellie, became my family. I felt she had adopted me into her family; loving and generous, she told everyone that I was her son. She bridged many gaps in my life.

The power of people who have a genuine love for caring and supporting others can't be gauged. I am so thankful to Ms. Landheart because she offered an immeasurable amount of support to me during a very difficult time in my life. Until I actually experienced Ms. Landheart's generosity, I had not known that people could be so kind enough to offer themselves and all that they have to someone they had only known for a short period of time. Ms. Landheart's gracious act totally changed my life and helped to shape my attitude for the work that I do today to impact the lives of others.

After staying with Ms. Landheart for two years, my mother found a home in the community where I attended school. In order for me to play varsity football, I needed to live with one of my legal guardians in the school district that I attended. My mother made the sacrifice because she wanted me to stay in the community where I had found so much support. I appreciated the sacrifice that my mother made and didn't want to let anyone down because so many people supported me along my journey. I would go on to have an excellent senior year athletically and academically.

"People who plan to make a difference in the world are willing to do so because of the love they have for others."

-Tyrone Smith

Neither of my parents graduated from high school, so graduating held a special significance in my family. As a senior at Willowridge High School, I was given an opportunity to tour local elementary schools in the district and to encourage the students to strive for success. My teachers and coaches chose me to be one of the speakers for the district-wide achievement tour because of my strong academic and athletic record, and for the positive way that I carried myself on and off the football field. I felt honored to have been chosen as a high school student to speak to elementary students about my journey. That experience laid the foundation for the work that I do to empower students today.

During the district-wide achievement tour, I spoke to students at five different elementary school campuses. Our last visit was to Ridgemont Elementary, the school that I attended when my family moved to Missouri City. I asked to speak specifically to Mrs. Williams' fifth grade class. I wanted to thank her for her love and encouragement during a pivotal time in my life. She had taken the time not only to listen, but also to instill in me a greater sense of self-control. She provided the encouragement and understanding that I did not have the year before in fourth grade. There weren't enough words to express my appreciation to her. When she hugged me that day, I was once again that fifth grade boy that desperately needed someone to understand him. Seven years later, there she was, influencing her students to choose a better path just as she had done with me. Looking back, I am acutely aware of how instrumental Mrs. Williams and others were in shaping me into the man I am today.

One of the greatest lessons that I learned from Mrs. Williams is that the more you believe in yourself, the more powerful you are as a person. No one can stomp on your dreams, and no one can make you less than what you are, *unless* you allow it. That is why the choice to be an achiever or a doubter starts with you. Doubters give up too easily on themselves because they look to others to define who they are. When others have a negative view of them, they believe that it must be true and they do nothing to change it. Achievers know that no matter what anyone else thinks, they are capable of greatness. Similar to the message that Coach Brantley gave me years later, you must remember that you cannot always choose the people who come into your life, but you can choose their place in your life. Make sure you choose well.

Coach Brantley's words, "Make sure you choose well," resonated with me as I crossed paths with a beautiful young lady while in college at Baylor University. DeMonica, who also happened to be an accomplished athlete, was very passionate about helping others while at Baylor. Within the first month of knowing her, I knew that she was a giver and someone who was willing to make an impact on the world. DeMonica and I grew to be the best of friends, and I took my time getting to know her as a person.

Many times people do not take the time to get to know one another, and by not doing so, they have regrets years after a relationship has already been established. In getting to know DeMonica, I realized that we had some of the same goals and aspirations. We shared a passion to do more and reach for greatness. With DeMonica being one of the nation's most recognized and recruited sprinters out of high school, and with me being the underdog and "never quit" football player, our lives meshed because we both knew what it meant to work and commit to something bigger in life. We both knew that as athletes, we were given a platform to make a difference in the lives of others by using our influence. We also both believed that even if we did not get the opportunity to play at a higher level in the sports that we loved, our educations were even more valuable. Cognizant that our educations would last a lifetime, we propelled one another to excel and committed ourselves to our educations. DeMonica helped me to understand the importance of surrounding yourself with people who will challenge you, uplift you and push you to be better; this is what DeMonica did, and still does, for me.

DeMonica and I have been married for nineteen years. I can say that it is an honor and a blessing to have her as my wife, friend, and partner. Together, we have used our influence to work in schools and churches, on community projects, and with many other organizations to impact the lives of others. We have made a commitment to our union in marriage, and have made a mutual commitment to make a difference in the world. When I started First and Goal, Inc., DeMonica enthusiastically and without question joined me for the journey. Wholeheartedly, we directed our efforts at being agents for change. Through our daily work together, we've seen the importance of building each other up and maintaining a quality family unit. Our relationship, from the time that we were in college to the present-day, has helped me to realize the importance of choosing the right people for your life. I think that as you grow and move forward in life, you should take a self inventory, including identifying the type of people that you want to surround yourself with. These people should be a reflection of you.

Everyone likes to be surrounded by people who understand them, people who can relate to them. Human beings want to feel understood. There is a sense of security when you hear a friend say, "I get what you are saying. I understand you." They understand us, and they understand what we have been through. In truth, the simple fact that they understand what you are saying, thinking, or feeling silently encourages you to continue. So, the next step is to choose your surroundings, to choose your friends, and to choose your influences. We were all placed on this earth to coexist; life would not be meaningful without the people who shape the world around us.

· · · · **•** • · · ·

KEY POINT:

❖ We each have a sphere of influence; the challenge is to use our influence in the right way.

KEY ACTION:

❖ Surround yourself with positive people and choose to be an achiever.

"Our influence can be used to make a great difference in the world, but only if we use it in the right way."

- Tyrone Smith: Outside the Huddle

OUTSIDE

the

HUDDLE

Steps to Developing a Game Plan for Life

OUTSIDE *the* HUDDLE

Steps to Developing a Game Plan for Life

PLAN

. . . . . . ● . . . . .

"Purpose without a plan is failure."

-Tyrone Smith

hen you first think of an idea, what do you do? Do you immediately fantasize about the idea becoming a reality, or do you immediately go to work with no clear direction? If your answer was "yes" to either question, your life may need a plan. A dream will remain a dream if you do not create a plan to make it a reality. You can easily say that you are going to become the greatest scholar, entertainer, or professional, but it takes work to get there; you must plan. Be willing to chase your dreams by creating a plan to succeed in life, regardless of what others think or say.

When I was younger, I thought that I had it all figured out and knew my plan for my life. Being from the inner city, one of my deepest desires was to become an entertainer. Yes, I dreamed of one day becoming this phenomenal rapper that would sell millions of albums worldwide. I dreamed about traveling the world and having sold out concerts. I shared my dream with my friends, but they did not see what I saw.

Tyrone, how can you become a rapper, and you can barely spell?

Tyrone, you can't be a famous rapper because you truly have no skills.

Jay Z, I don't think so. But Jay No, I can see because you have no skills.

Ouch, that really hurt! So then I thought maybe I could become a professional wrestler like Hulk Hogan or Dwayne "The Rock" Johnson. I would wake up on Saturday mornings ready to watch professional wrestling with only underwear on and a towel wrapped around my shoulders as a cape. I would then say, "I am thinking in my mind who will be destroyed today!" Next I would hear:

Tyrone, you are too small!
Tyrone, you are too skinny!
Tyrone, you are not big enough!

Ouch, that hurt too! I would respond, "You mean to tell me that I can't be like Dwayne 'The Rock' Johnson and say, 'Can you smell what The Rock is cooking?'" My friends would say, "No." I'd say, "You mean to tell me that I can't be like John Cena, flashing all five fingers in front of my face, saying, 'You can't see me?'"

And of course my friends again would say, "No," and repeat:

Tyrone, you are too small!
Tyrone, you are too skinny!
Tyrone, you are not big enough!

I then figured that my greatest plan would be to become a professional football player. My friends bashed that plan, too.

Tyrone, you are too small and too skinny.
You are not big enough.
You are not fast enough.
You are not good enough.
You are not cute enough.
You have a big head, and you cry all of the time!

Ouch, that hurt even more! I often struggled with what

others had to say about me as a person. The problem was I placed too much value on the opinions of others. At this time in my life, I was not aware of who I was as a person, so other people's opinions and thoughts mattered to me. Their opinions mattered to me because I wanted to be accepted. I was still trying to find myself, and all that I could become in life. I had few friends growing up, so I wanted to fit in. I later had to realize that everyone did not have my best interest in mind; I had to get to a point where I valued my life regardless of what others had to say. Other people had their opinions and plans for my life, but I had to recognize that only I had the power to make my plans a reality. If you can get to a point where you truly love yourself and do not care what others think of you, then you will begin to grow internally. You will know that you matter as a person and that your life is what you make it.

Other people may have certain thoughts or feelings about you as a person, but what is most important is how you feel about yourself. People may think little of themselves and would like you to think little of yourself because they have no true purpose or drive for their life. There is a saying that describes this attitude: "Misery loves company." Another person cannot live out your dreams, goals or hopes; therefore, it is up to you to be driven to succeed. You must not let the insecurities of others stop you from putting your plan into action. Do not let others count you out; you are destined to be great.

Most of the time, we let external factors shape how big we dream and ultimately how we plan. We let external things limit our reach, but we must realize our internal greatness. We all have it in us to dream big and to make an impact as long as we remember the following things:

1. Count yourself in. You are destined to be great.
2. Ignore others' opinions. Your life is not shaped by their opinions.
3. Take positive action. You must invest in your dreams.
4. Keep the dream alive. You must be willing to continue dreaming.

A dream is just a dream if you are not willing to take action to make it a reality. As you think about the many things that you have dreamed about and desire to do in life, it is key that you first think about *how* you can make your dreams a reality. The first step is to set a goal in regard to your overall plan for achieving what you desire. Setting goals is essential for the success of all individuals, teams, projects, and organizations. It is not just about dreaming big. You have to set short-term and long-term goals as well.

Once you have set your goals, next establish a plan of action to achieve the goals. Your plan must outline how you will achieve the goals and objectives that you desire for your life. It is up to you to execute each step that will draw you closer to your desired outcome. Action on your part is required to make any dream or goal a reality. What steps are you willing to take?

. . . . ● ● . . . .

If your destination is success, then failure will not be an option. You must be willing to dedicate yourself and make the necessary sacrifices. Your willingness to work hard is essential to making any plan successful. Remember that every plan requires action.

I learned about the importance of work the summer that I was eleven years old. By nine o'clock in the morning, the summer heat was fierce and unrelenting. I would pause just long enough to mop the sweat from my forehead with a rag while pushing the lawnmower through my yard. With every push of the lawnmower through the grassy forest of our yard, I could hear my mother's voice echoing in my head.

"You are too little and skinny to play football, Tyrone," she said after I asked her if I could play on the little league football team in the fall. "You will just get out there and get hurt."

My two older brothers, Harold, Jr. and Tusshun, mocked me as they took turns pretending to be me getting knocked unconscious by an invisible linebacker. "Listen to Mom!" they shouted. "Football is too tough a sport for you."

But I would not give up. Every day I badgered my mom to let me play. This was my chance to play real, organized football, not just two-hand touch in the street or three on three in the park. This was little league football with coaches and teammates. For the first time in my life, I would get to play the game that I loved, wearing the equipment of real athletes: a helmet, a mouth piece, shoulder pads, butt pads, thigh pads, and cleats; but in order to get that gear, I had to pay a sixty-dollar registration fee.

"I'm not paying sixty dollars just to watch my baby boy get knocked around," said my mother, exasperated by my begging. "If you want to play so much, then you pay for it yourself."

I knew that my mom thought that telling me to pay the fee myself would be the end of it. At eleven years old, sixty dollars was a fortune. My brothers and I were lucky to receive a few dollars from my dad to buy candy or soda from the corner store, and we would always share that money. There was no way, though, that my brothers would hand over their portions. Even if they did, three or four dollars every few weeks would not be enough to pay the full amount for the registration fee.

One day I sat on the top step of the front porch with my chin in my hand. I had to come up with a way to earn sixty dollars by the end of the summer! It was then that I saw my neighbor mowing his front lawn. As I watched him creating swatches with the mower through the tall grass, an idea came to me.

"Hello, Mr. Johnson!" I called to him, waving to get his attention over the buzzing mower. "Do you have a minute?"

"Hey there, Tyrone!" he said, turning off the mower. "What can I do for you?"

"I was wondering if I could cut your grass for you," I said. "I'm trying to raise money so I can play little league football in the fall."

"Hmm . . . well, how much you charging?" Mr. Johnson asked. I had already thought of my price before I crossed from my yard. The price needed to be a low enough amount to be worth it to him to let me cut the grass while he enjoyed his weekend. The sweltering Texas summer heat was unbearable, so I figured I could make decent money if I could get more of my neighbors to pay me to mow their yards.

"I charge five dollars to mow the front, another five for the back, and two dollars to sweep up the clippings," I said in a business-like fashion.

Mr. Johnson smiled and considered my offer for a moment. "Alright, Tyrone. I'll let you finish the front yard, cut the back and sweep up for me. If you do a good job, I'll pay you twelve dollars."

The yard looked like an unkempt forest of overgrown weeds, but I would earn twelve dollars to cut it; every penny made the job well worth the time.

> *Establish an overall plan for your life, and you*
> *will be much more likely to accomplish your goals.*
>
> *-Tyrone Smith*

After being paid for finishing Mr. Johnson's backyard, I went to a few of the other neighbors and asked if they would let me cut their grass for a small price. I got a few no's, but I also got enough yes's to earn the registration fee by the end of the summer. I cut and swept three yards that day, including Mr. Johnson's. By the end of the day, every muscle in my body ached, but I had earned thirty-six dollars! In one day, I was halfway to my goal. I had to keep it up for the rest of the summer, and in the fall I would be on the football field.

Mowing those lawns was grueling work. My back and shoulder muscles were always sore, even when I was not pushing the lawnmower. The sun beamed unsympathetically on my head, and my brothers joked that I was so dark from the sun that the streetlights came on when I walked outside. However, I ignored their jokes and kept to my plan.

At times, the temptation to spend the money was overwhelming. I would hear the ice cream truck coming down the street and would want to make a beeline for my savings. Or my favorite rapper would release a new album that I really wanted, and I again would be tempted to dip into my earnings. But I kept my goal in sight. A group of my friends would go to the local amusement park, and I would feel a wistful pang of regret because I had to miss out on a day of roller coasters and funnel cake. Still, I kept my goal in sight. Each time that I felt the urge to spend the money, I would imagine myself on the football field and refocus my attention on my goal. I was determined to make my dream a reality.

Finally, all of my planning, strategizing, and hard work paid off. By the end of the summer, I had earned the money that I needed to pay the registration fee. My mother had to admit that she had not believed that I could do it, but I remained committed to achieving my goal, and she was proud of me. Even though she still did not want me to play football, she felt that I had earned the opportunity to play the sport that I loved because I had worked so hard. By creating a plan and staying focused, I learned that I could accomplish something.

Anything worth having requires hard work. You must have a plan of action to achieve what you desire. To plan is to understand what it means to set goals for your life. From the time that I was twelve years old, I set a goal to play in the NFL. It was an eleven-year process, but my dream finally became a reality at the age of twenty-three. This happened only because I formed a plan of action and stayed focused.

．　．　．　＊　●　＊　．　．　．　．

There is a story about a man who went to the doctor because he was afraid that he might be dying. He told the doctor that every time he touched his head, it hurt; every time he touched his stomach, it hurt; and every time he touched his leg, it hurt. The doctor examined him and told him that he had some good news and some bad news. The good news was that he was not dying. The bad news was that he had a broken finger! Here is a man who needed to learn how to focus.

Like the man in the story, we sometimes focus on all of the wrong things. Being able to focus on the bigger picture helps us to understand that some processes are essential parts of creating a plan for success. A person with a plan is not just floating through life waiting for something to happen; a person with a plan *creates* his path instead of reacting to the path that others create for him. If you establish an overall plan for your life, you will be much more likely to accomplish your goals, mainly because YOU plan to succeed.

Are you ready to start creating a plan to accomplish your goals? If so, think about what it will take to accomplish those goals and start writing down the steps. Focus on these steps and from now on, choose to take action! Follow your plan every day, knowing that you will not fail because YOU are destined to succeed!

· · · · ● ● ● · · · ·

KEY POINT:

◆ It is crucial that you plan in order to make your dreams a reality. Once that plan is established, follow the plan and chase your dreams daily.

KEY ACTION:

◆ What steps are you taking to make your dreams a reality?

"As you think about the many things that you have dreamed about and desire to do in life, it is key that you first think about how you can make your dreams a reality."

- Tyrone Smith: Outside the Huddle

OUTSIDE
the
HUDDLE

OUTSIDE the HUDDLE

Steps to Developing a Game Plan for Life

PROCESS

· · · · · ● · · · ·

"Success is a process, not a destination."

-Tyrone Smith

The process is the manner in which we work to see the big picture in life. What is it that you are working toward? Are you keeping the big picture and overall goal in mind as you embrace the process? Keeping your goal in mind will prepare you to persevere and overcome failure. According to Merriam-Webster, *perseverance* is the quality that allows someone to continue trying to do something even though it is difficult. *You will need perseverance in order to go through the process.* Through all of the obstacles, roadblocks, and setbacks that I have encountered in life, it has been rewarding to know that I embraced those moments as opportunities for real growth. Remember that pain, failure, growth, and maturity are a part of the process. Once you realize that you can grow from failed experiences in life, it enables you to mature and learn to embrace the process.

So often in life, people focus on the destination rather than the journey; but it is the journey through life that truly shapes us as individuals. Our growth and development during the journey toward our successes are a part of the process that helps define who we are. If we would just learn to embrace the moment, we would be more satisfied with the end result of our process. You will find that what you gain during the process is just as valuable as what you are trying to achieve. The process will shape, develop and mature you, and no matter how long it takes, every step of the process will be well worth it.

· · · · * ● * · · · ·

The process is rarely what we expect it to be. I experienced this firsthand in the seventh grade. For me, one of the most exciting events in seventh grade was finally being able to join the football team. Only seventh and eighth graders were allowed to participate in school sports, and for this reason, my friends and I spent most of our sixth grade year looking forward to becoming seventh graders. When the time finally came for football tryouts, I was one of the first to sign up. The football team was divided into the A Team and the B Team. Everyone's goal was to make the A Team because they were considered the best players. My friends and I teased one another about who would make the A Team and who would be put on the B Team, all the while boasting about our abilities to run fast and hit hard when we tackled someone.

As tryouts began, I was determined to showcase my skills. I knew that I was a front-runner for the A Team. I boasted to my friends that I was one of the best, and I convinced myself that I was already the best football player in middle school history. Even though I had barely played football, no one could tell me that I could not tackle like Ray Lewis, run like Darryl Green, or score a touchdown like Jerry Rice. I was positive that the coaches were watching me, in awe of my natural talent. I had played little league football the previous year with the Windsor Redskins, so I felt like I was ready for junior high football. I was totally focused and keyed in during the tryouts, sprinting like a deer through the cone drills, catching every pass thrown my way, and making vicious tackles during the tackling drills. I felt there was nothing else to prove to the coaches when it came to my talent and tenacity for the game. I liked my execution during the tryouts and was sure I had secured my spot on the A Team.

I arrived at school early on the day that the coach was to

announce who made the football team. As soon as I saw the postings on the locker room wall, I began searching the A Team players for my name. I ran my finger down the paper over and over again, looking for my name. I kept telling myself that I was overlooking it. Somewhere around the fifteenth time searching for my name on the list, I realized that *Tyrone Smith* was not on the A Team. Reluctantly, I looked over to the B Team sheet. As I stared at my name, I was devastated. During the tryouts, the B Team had not really existed for me. I was so certain that I was going to be on the A Team that the thought of making the B Team never entered my mind. A part of me wanted to quit right then and there.

I thought that the coaches obviously could not spot true talent, so I wondered why I should waste my time playing for them. But I loved the game of football too much to give up. I loved running and making plays, but most of all I loved being allowed to hit someone as hard as I could without getting into trouble. Football was my outlet, my controlled chaos, and I did not want to stop playing for any reason. There was no way that I would ever be satisfied playing for the B Team, but I had to if I wanted to continue playing football.

As the season progressed, I became more and more disheartened as I played on the B Team. I was truly affected by not making the A Team, and I dwelled on it often. I knew that I was just as good, if not better, than some of the kids playing on the A Team. I felt that the coaches had chosen their favorites instead of picking the better players, and it made me resentful. At the time, I did not understand that the skills in my mind and what I was actually doing on the field were two very different things. I was trying to imitate all of my favorite professional players instead of doing what my coaches wanted me to do.

I would try to tell myself to wait for next year, but eighth grade felt like a long way off and there was a chance that the coaches still would not pick me. Instead of playing harder to prove myself, I began doing the bare minimum in practice. That attitude transferred over to my schoolwork, and my grades spiraled downward. Around this time, Texas passed a new law, House Bill 72—well known as "No Pass, No Play." House Bill 72 came in response to a growing concern over deteriorating literacy among Texas schoolchildren over two decades, which was reflected in students' scores on standardized tests. It prohibited students who were failing classes from participating in sports and other extracurricular activities for a six-week period.

Even though I knew that I was not working as hard as I could in class, I thought that I was doing enough to get by . . . until I found out that I was failing Ms. Bigelow's math class. Because of the new law, I would miss the final three weeks of football. In a sense, I had failed off the football team. For the first time in my life, I had failed and consequently had lost something valuable to me. Even playing for the B Team was now better than not playing at all.

The day I found out that I had failed and could no longer play, I participated in one final practice with my team and coaches. I never practiced so hard in my life. I ran faster and tackled harder, trying to release some of my anger and sadness on the field. My stomach was tied up in knots, and for the first time I felt a real fear that I might become a failure. Worst of all, I did not know how to make that feeling go away.

When I arrived home earlier than usual from school the next day, my dad asked me why I was not at football practice. I had not told my parents about failing my math class. I knew that they would find out as soon as my report card arrived, but my dad could tell that I was keeping something from him. He questioned me again about why I was home from school so early.

"I failed off the football team and can't play anymore," I mumbled under my breath. My dad made me repeat what I said twice before he heard it clearly enough to understand me.

"You failed off the football team?" He stared at me while I studied the floor, trying not to meet his eyes. He knew how much football meant to me, and he could see that I was already feeling the consequences of my actions. Finally, he sighed and shook his head.

"Well, how do you feel about that?" he asked.

"I don't feel good about it," I said, still studying the floor.

"You don't?"

"No." I looked up at him and felt all of the hurt bubbling up inside of me. "I don't feel good about flunking a class and being a failure, and now I can't play football anymore this year."

"Then I want you to remember this moment," my dad said. "Remember how you feel right now, and if you don't want to ever feel this way again, take care of your business." That was all that he said about the matter, but it was enough to stay with me for the rest of my life.

> *"Then I want you to remember this moment," my dad said. "Remember how you feel right now, and if you don't want to ever feel this way again, take care of your business."*
>
> *- Harold Smith, Sr.*

From that experience, I learned the difference between personal failure and having a failed experience. We all have failed experiences, no matter how hard we try to avoid them. However, achievers learn from failures by realizing that they are part of the process. During the journey, we may stumble and fall, but one of the truest measures of personal achievement is the determination to keep going following a failed attempt. Henry Ford once said, *"Failure is only the opportunity to begin again more intelligently."* I realized that my education was the key to my success, and not making it my priority was only hurting me and keeping me from my goals. By not doing my best, I was only failing myself.

I truly appreciate the understanding and growth that accompanied the process of my journey in mathematics. I had been a fourth grader struggling with multiplication and division; then I failed Ms. Bigelow's math class in the seventh grade and was dismissed from the football team, but that wasn't the end of the process. I grew to enjoy math, and it became one of my favorite subjects. My math teachers in high school, Mr. Emery and Mr. Price, loved my approach and attention to detail in class. They didn't know that my previous failed experiences in math are what led me to appreciate math so much. The failures that I experienced were setbacks, but I did not let them stop me from making a comeback and gaining a greater sense of my journey in life. Once you realize that you can grow from setbacks, it becomes a testament to your maturity. I grew to understand that the journey is where true strength comes from.

* * * * * * * * * *

After failing off the football team in the seventh grade, I learned to truly embrace every part of the process, including the failures. It motivated and inspired me to realize that through it all I needed to continue to press on because the journey was going to be grueling at times, but it would be key in making my dreams a reality. That failed experience provided my initial life lesson in embracing the process, and learning that I could control my attitude and outlook while making the most of my opportunities. In the eighth grade I made the B Team again, but I did not get discouraged because I knew this too was a part of the process.

In the ninth grade, I was not always the fastest or biggest kid, and my body was not fully developed. I once overhead a coach tell another coach that he felt that I was not developed enough physically, and I was not mature enough to play on the varsity team for football or track. When I heard those comments I was hurt, but I knew that I had control of my effort. So, once again I waited my turn. I was more determined to succeed and to take this moment as a personal challenge to work harder, get stronger, and leave no room for doubt. I had no control over what team I was placed on, but I had control over my effort and the way that I practiced as an athlete. I also learned that the same effort, drive, and passion that I used in football could be practiced in the classroom as well. I went to study hall after school, I asked my teachers questions, and I connected with student-led study groups because I wanted to practice good habits in all things. If you desire to be the best, you should have a desire to do your best in *everything* that you do. If you practice being great in all that you do, I can assure you that you will be successful in life.

During my senior year in high school, all of my hard work and patience finally paid off. I was finally on the varsity team, and it was a year that I will never forget. My journey had led me to become a student of embracing every step of the process, and an even greater student of increasing my skills and endurance. I practiced with a tireless work ethic as a result of all of the things that I had to overcome. My work ethic and drive could not be tested because I learned to practice at a high level. I was preparing myself for when my moment came, and when that moment did come, I was ready to handle my business on the football field.

I was a true shut down cornerback my senior year. I was taking out all opposition defensively at cornerback, and I was driven to nullify anyone that came on my side of the field. I played with an unbelievable confidence because I consistently gave it my all and practiced at a high level in order to maximize my opportunities. This was evident during my first football game as a starter. We played Stratford High School in the season opener on a fall Friday night under the lights at Tully Stadium. It was my first varsity football game; I was excited, yet calm at the same time. The journey had been long and grueling, but I was ready to let my light shine that night. I played with so much passion and confidence; it was as if I had already been playing on the varsity team since my freshman year. We dominated Stratford High School and won our opening game my senior year, and to build on the moment, I was featured in the sports section of the *Houston Chronicle* and *Houston Post* the following morning. My senior football season was incredible; no wide receiver caught a pass on me over twenty yards, and no wide receiver caught a touchdown on me the entire season. I was playing like one of my greatest heroes on the field, Deon "Prime Time" Sanders. During my journey, everything that I faced, every failure, prepared me for that moment of greatness. Going through the process strengthened me both physically and mentally. My senior year was filled with victories, both on and off the field, because I embraced the process and continuously grew from my earlier years of failed experiences.

* * * * ● * * * *

During college I learned another lesson in embracing the process. While at Baylor University, Coach Bob Cope was my defensive back coach during my sophomore year. He was very critical of the way that I played and often challenged me to do better. It was sometimes very hard to accept the things that he had to say about my performance on the field. I soon realized that the reason he was so tough on me was because he saw greatness in me and wanted me to reach my full potential. I remember Coach Cope telling me many times during practice that if I would trust what he was telling me to do, I would one day play in the National Football League. Coach Cope saw something in me that I did not see in myself. At the time, I was just a player that was content with being a starter on the college level. However, he saw me as more than a college player; he saw me as a professional player. Coach Cope believed that I would eventually grow into something more; I just had to be willing to take from the criticism and accept the process.

Others may see something in you that you do not see in yourself, so you must be open to embracing constructive criticism as another part of the growth process. Constructive criticism is not meant to hurt you, but instead to further develop you as a person. As hard as it was to hear criticism from Coach Cope, I understood that it was to make me better. Just as I had to trust myself, I also had to build trust in others during my journey. We cannot see the possibilities that lie ahead, but the process grants us the strength to trust in the wisdom of others. Accepting constructive criticism is yet another necessary part of improving ourselves along the journey of life.

* * * * * * * * * *

I believe that we all can embrace the process of life as a genuine opportunity to grow, because there will be many teachable moments along the way. A good friend of mine, Dr. Xavier Whitaker, would always make the following statement: "Life is filled with teachable moments." However, life is filled with teachable moments only if you perceive them as teachable. In addition, the challenge is how you respond to life being filled with teachable moments, not just the moments themselves. If you embrace the moment by understanding and applying its life lesson in order to achieve a desired goal, then the moment will be teachable. You should embrace the process and know that there is a reward at the end if you continue to persevere, trust, and believe.

· · · · · ● · · · ·

KEY POINT:

- Realize that success is a process and that life is an ever-changing journey. Be willing to adapt while remaining committed to your goals.

KEY ACTION:

- Embrace the process. You are destined to be great, but you also must be true to yourself.

"If we would just learn to embrace the moment that we are in, we would be a lot more satisfied with the end result of our process."

- Tyrone Smith: Outside the Huddle

OUTSIDE
the
HUDDLE

Steps to Developing a Game Plan for Life

OUTSIDE *the* HUDDLE

Steps to Developing a Game Plan for Life

PRACTICE

· · · · · ● · · · ·

"To live a full life, you must get to know your inner truth. Understanding your weaknesses will encourage your strengths. Acknowledging your limitations can help you better focus on what motivates you."

-Tyrone Smith

Many of us have heard the saying, "Good things in life never come easily." It is true that the good things or anything worth having in life will require a certain level of commitment and enthusiasm. In order to live your life committed to a purpose, you must practice habits that will allow you to succeed. I have never seen anyone accomplish anything in life without some form of method or commitment. Life will require you to push yourself daily in school, at home, at work and in the community; so learning the importance of practicing good habits is vital in every aspect of your life. Think about your life and how much better it would be if you prepared and practiced with your purpose, goals, and dreams in mind. If you give your best in everything, whether you succeed or fail, you will have the satisfaction of knowing that you did all you could by practicing and preparing. By practicing good habits, you are taking the necessary steps toward true fulfillment in life.

Before reading any further, I would like you to think about the following question: *what is practice?* For me, practice means a lot of things. It means to repeat an action over and over again to become better; it means to improve; and it means to train your body and mind in such a way that ultimately, the activity becomes a part of your life. Only then will you gain discipline, through which comes commitment.

In the previous section on Process, I revealed how my failure to make the A Team in seventh grade influenced me to make bad decisions that drove me off of the football team. However, through that experience I began to understand how it takes both success and failure to shape us as individuals and form the processes through which we achieve our goals. During the eighth grade, I was more determined than ever to overcome my failures and to make the A Team.

I began the eighth grade at a new school, Christa McAuliffe Middle School. What a perfect opportunity for a clean slate, in a new school with different coaches! I was determined to make the A Team during football tryouts, but when the teams were posted, I found my name was on the B Team list once again. This time, instead of blaming the coaches, I evaluated myself and honed in on what I was doing wrong. I did not prepare properly during the summer. I was eating a lot of junk food. I was not practicing my catching drills, and I was not even running enough to ensure that I would be in shape.

I realized that I was an average size and not the fastest kid on the team. I began to feel like I would never be good enough to make it on the A Team. Even though I practiced, deep down I knew that I was doing just enough to be on the football team. I lacked dedication and drive, and I was not putting forth any extra effort. My practice and preparation were not the best. My grades remained high enough to continue participating in sports, but otherwise I was the same middle-of-the-pack kid I had been in my previous school.

At this point in my life, I had no idea what it meant to practice and to commit to something by giving it my all. I lacked the drive and engagement to be better because I did not understand the value of practice, or how it could change my life in every capacity. I would soon find out that my level of commitment was the missing element. Once football season ended, many of my teammates joined the track team, and I decided to do the same. I did not enjoy running track as much as tackling on the football field. However, it gave me something to do in the off-season, and I hoped that track and field would make me faster for football. My track coach was Dennis Brantley, who had been my history teacher and one of my football coaches. At the time, Coach Brantley was also a professional athlete and competed in track and field events. When he was not coaching or teaching, he was practicing and training for competition.

He pushed us to become better athletes just as hard as he pushed himself. Sometimes we would grumble and complain that we were not professional athletes like him, but Coach Brantley never let up on us. Instead, if he heard us complaining, he would make our training sessions more challenging. Coach Brantley told us that we would get out of practice what we put into it, nothing more and nothing less. He also offered to train us during extra hours on weekends. Those practices were not mandatory, but he emphasized how important they would be if we were serious about becoming better athletes.

> *"Acknowledging your limitations can help you better focus on what motivates you."*
>
> *- Tyrone Smith*

At first, those weekend practices included most of the team, but as time passed it dwindled to just a few of us. At the time, I was not sure why I continued with it. Track and field was not the sport I loved, but Coach Brantley inspired me to remain committed. A large part of it was seeing how committed he was. Through Coach Brantley, I learned what it meant to be passionate about my goals and how to dedicate myself to achieving them. Coach Brantley would often tell me that it did not matter whether I was the biggest, fastest, or strongest. He said that as long as I was willing to work hard, I was capable of accomplishing great things. He made me believe it, and I was ready to follow his direction and put in the work.

That spring in the eighth grade, words like commitment, passion, drive, and determination began to take on a special meaning. Coach Brantley never let me lose focus, and he helped me overcome my doubts in myself and in my abilities. He became more than my coach; he also became a mentor and a friend. He trained me all through the spring and summer, and continued to work with me even after I left Christa McAuliffe Middle School to attend Willowridge High School. Even with Coach Brantley training me, I still did not make it on the varsity football team until my senior year in high school. Coach Brantley continuously encouraged me and helped me to realize that even though I could not immediately see the improvement in my skills, it did not mean that I was not growing. I had to learn to trust that my hard work would eventually pay off. He pushed me to never give up and to keep practicing and working on my athletic skills.

It was not only my athletic skills that were improving, though. All of this hard work was reflected in my academic performance as well. Developing a strong work ethic made me realize that I had to invest time in my studies to become academically successful, and I continued to apply this work ethic during the following school years. During my junior and senior years in high school, I was committed to preparing for college and to performing well on the SAT/ACT as a result of the work ethic that I developed in middle school.

The most important lesson that I learned from Coach Brantley was that nothing worth having comes easily. My efforts truly paid off during my senior year of high school when I received over fifty Division-1 scholarship offers for football from various colleges. I was awarded an athletic scholarship to Baylor University; I was the starting cornerback from my sophomore to senior season, and chosen as a team captain. I graduated with my Bachelor of Arts degree in Sociology and ultimately played professional football in the NFL.

At each level of accomplishment, I still maintained the same work ethic. At Baylor University, although we were only required to train once a day during the summer, I practiced twice daily to improve my skills. I also stayed committed to excelling in school. During my rookie year in the NFL, I trained every day, even on Christmas Day. The knowledge that I acquired through practice benefited me not only in athletics, but in every area of my life. No matter what skill or talent you may have, you must work hard if you want to excel. It will require a lot of time and effort, but hard work and a determined mind will always benefit you in the end.

> *"I've always considered myself to be just average talent and what I have is a ridiculous insane obsessiveness for practice and preparation.""*
>
> *- Will Smith*

HARD WORK + DETERMINATION = JERRY RICE

> *"Prepare and practice as if the game was today."*
>
> *-Jim Mora, Jr.*

Jerry Rice is considered the best wide receiver in the history of the National Football League, and I am not just saying this because he was one of my teammates from the San Francisco 49ers. His approach, work ethic, and the way he practiced the game of football was extraordinary to witness up close and personal.

Jerry Rice's father was a bricklayer. When Jerry was a young boy, he often worked with his father and experienced his father's daily commitment to hard work. At a young age, he realized that the capacity for hard work would give him positive results in life, and he later applied this ideology to his own career. He trained at an amazingly high level in preparation for the games each week; even in practice, you could see the greatness of Jerry Rice in motion each day. Being a defensive back, I had many opportunities to defend Jerry Rice during practice. It was an honor knowing that I was defending the best wide receiver in the NFL. I was most impressed with the way that he practiced and his commitment to becoming better, even though he was already considered the best.

After each pass he caught in practice, he would sprint to the end zone on the other end of the field. It did not matter if the end zone was 20, 30, 40, 50, or 80 yards away, he would sprint at full speed. Yes, he would do this in practice everyday. At that time, Jerry was an All-Pro, a perennial Pro Bowl player, and had already won three Super Bowl rings. Even though he had made all of these accomplishments, he still practiced at the highest level. Some days Jerry would stay after practice to do additional work, and I was always willing to work with him. I watched Jerry carefully and learned what it takes to be a champion. I saw that his success as an athlete began with the way he approached practice every day. If you want to be great, you always have to be willing to practice at a great level.

Jerry Rice approached the game of football with excellence, not mediocrity. If we learn to commit to everything in life with a high level of excellence, drive, and dedication, we will accomplish greatness as individuals. Your life will be filled with opportunities, but you must be willing to make the necessary commitments in order to take full advantage of these opportunities. I believe that having a greater desire to succeed will motivate you to give greater effort. There is no substitute for hard work, so you have to be willing to push yourself if you want to improve. You must be true to your grind because anything worth having requires passion, drive, commitment, and practice. If you are willing to practice and dedicate yourself to whatever it is that you desire, you are preparing yourself to succeed in life.

Practice Makes Perfect.

"Focus on developing practical habits for success."

-Tyrone Smith

We have all heard the old adage, "Practice makes PERFECT." This saying applies in life and on the journey to success. Everyday habits greatly influence either the successes or failures of an individual. A commitment to excellence in everything we do must be a daily habit that we go out of our way to achieve.

You can build a commitment to practice by first realizing that the goals you have set for yourself will require you to work/practice. You must understand that the work you are willing to put in is based on your commitment and discipline. You can practice effectively by developing a routine that supports your desired goals. Such a routine requires you to do the following:

1. Commit to practice a dedicated amount of time each day. It will take time to get better at anything in life, but you will not get better if you do not put in the time.

2. Evaluate your results based on the amount of time that you have committed to practice. Are you getting better or seeing improvements? If so, remember to use your improvements, no matter how big or small, as motivation to continue toward your goal.

3. If you are not seeing the desired results, develop a plan of action to adjust your commitment to practice. Ask yourself . . . "Do I need to work harder? Do I need to dedicate more time each day to achieve my desired goals?" You have to be willing to ask yourself these hard questions when it comes to increasing your level of commitment, because you know yourself better than anyone.

4. Build consistency. You have to be consistent with the level of commitment that you have set for yourself. Of the 365 days in the year, how many days will you commit to practicing or doing what it takes to achieve your goals? Being consistent will make it easier to remain committed.

Remember, "Practice makes perfect." Keep practicing; keep dreaming; keep wishing to go further. You must be willing to work toward your goals if you want to achieve them. Make a daily commitment to be excellent. Honor this commitment to be the best that you can be, to be a self-starter, and to never give up. Your goals will require your drive, strength, commitment, and above it all, your practice. Get the practice in to make your goals a reality.

* * * * ● ● * * * *

KEY POINT:

◆ Anything in life worth having will take drive, strength, commitment and practice. You must be willing to work.

KEY ACTION:

◆ Practice positive habits in your life and work to develop your skills.

"I learned that if you want to be great, you always have to do extra work."

- Tyrone Smith: Outside the Huddle

OUTSIDE
the
HUDDLE

Steps to Developing a Game Plan for Life

OUTSIDE the HUDDLE

Steps to Developing a Game Plan for Life

PROGRESS

· · · · · ● · · · ·

"It's not where you start in life, but where you finish. Progress is a key component in measuring success. Progress can be measured in many ways."

-Tyrone Smith

We all have within us the desire to be greater and to do more than we have done before. Progress is made only when we make a genuine effort toward our goals, while at the same time keeping our purpose in focus. We must be willing to develop a plan of action to accomplish our purpose, because progress is moving from where you are to where you want to be. A fundamental truth about progress is that it begins by taking the first step. Progress is never determined by your limitations, but by your ability to look back and to see that you are farther from where you were when you began your journey. Anything that you have done to reach a new place along your journey is defined as progress.

When I realized that my purpose in life was to make a difference in the lives of others, I did not need anyone to validate the work that I was inspired to do, and that encouraged me to get up each day and forge ahead. People often told me that I would not accomplish a lot in life because I did not come from the best community; I did not come from a perfect household; I was not smart enough; and I was not big enough to play football. In my opinion, these are the types of circumstances from which you progress the most. Your desire in life should be to become a better person today than you were yesterday. How can you appreciate how far you have come if you did not have far to go?

I recently took my two sons, Tyrone II and Tyler, to Third Ward, the inner city of Houston where I was born and raised. I wanted to show them the homes that I lived in so that they could have an idea of my past and the journey that I have taken in life. As I have indicated, the homes that I lived in when I was younger were not in the best area of Houston, but I wanted to fully expose my sons to my journey and allow them to see the tremendous growth in my life. We drove up to the dilapidated old house, and as I stared at it so many memories of my childhood came flooding back to me. The house seemed so large to me when my brothers and I would chase one another from room to room playing tag and hide and seek. Now with the doors and windows boarded and the walls barely standing, I wondered how my parents were able to make such a small space into a comfortable and loving home. We exited the car and as my boys played and threw sticks from the sidewalk, I stood so lost in my thoughts that I barely noticed when an older man approached us.

"You can't be here," The older man said as he walked up to us. "This is private property." I looked at the man and immediately recognized him from my childhood. He was our former landlord, Mr. McAfee.

"Mr. McAfee! How are you? I'm Tyrone Smith, you may not remember me but my family used to live in this house." I explained to him that I had grown up there and even though he couldn't remember me at first, he did recall my parents. I told him that I wanted to show my childhood home to my kids and I introduced them to him. He shook each of their hands and looked back at me.

"You're here showing your boys where you come from?" he asked.

"Yes Sir," I said. "I want them to see where I started out."

Mr. McAfee nodded. "You take your time then, that's

important for them to see." He said. "They need to know." There was a solemnness in his tone as he looked around, taking in the neighborhood with me. It was apparent that we both were remembering a better time, before years of poverty and neglect had robbed the neighborhood of its dignity. As we stood staring at the dilapidated property together, he nodded again and repeated his words. "It's important for them to see this." Then he walked away.

I know that all of my experiences in life have shaped and matured me, and allowed me to recognize that my past is a testament of the progress that I have made in life. I want my children to understand that progress, and I don't want to ever forget. I dedicate so much of my life to giving back to this community because I feel that it is of the utmost importance. Knowing what it means to give back, with your humble beginnings still in mind, is true progress.

· · · · ● · · · · ·

Progress equals growth when you can look back and examine your personal growth and reflect on the changes you have made. One of the greatest challenges that I faced each day was the fear of the unknown. For me, the fear of the unknown involved the expectation of accomplishing something that had never been done in my family. Even with a cloud of fear hanging over my head, I had to come to the realization that I had something to offer the world. I couldn't let that fear stop me from moving forward in life; I couldn't let it hinder my progress.

When I left to attend college at Baylor University, I was stepping into the unknown. My fear was heightened because the experience of college life was totally new for me and my family. Neither my mother nor father finished high school, so they didn't have any experiences to share with me to ease my anxiety or lift that cloud of fear. The fear wasn't because I was leaving home for the first time; the fear stemmed from my overwhelming desire to not fail. No one in my family had ever gone to college before; no one in my family could tell me what I needed to do in order to accomplish what I was setting out to do. It was the unknown, and I was terrified.

My mother dropped me off at Baylor University and she had no idea what to say to me other than, "Respect others and don't get in trouble." Those few powerful words escalated the fear that I would have to conquer as a first generation college student. There I was, alone at a prestigious university, not believing that I was equipped or even ready for the challenge ahead. Although I thought that I was ready for college when I visited earlier in the year, there was a big difference between visiting a campus for two days and living there for four to five years. I often wondered if I had made the right decision about going to college, and this doubt was triggered by my fear of the unknown.

During my first semester, I soon realized that I had the ability to be a first class college student and graduate from Baylor University. I began to apply the lessons I had learned throughout my life to my college life. I knew that I could not achieve my goals without hard work, so I made sure that I went to every class; I sat at the front of all my classes; I attended study sessions, and I met with my academic advisor weekly. All of these things contributed to my success in the classroom during my first year, but the weekly meetings with my academic advisor, Walter Abercrombie, are what really helped me to deal with my fear of the unknown. Walter had already gone down the path that I was pursuing; he was a former NFL player and Baylor University graduate. Through my weekly conversations with Walter, I could share my worries, my doubts, and my greatest fears about being the first in my family to go to college. It was a great challenge for me, and Walter reminded me at each meeting that I had the capacity to do amazing things in life; the biggest thing that I needed was to be on my own, and I needed to forget the fears of being inadequate. I needed to believe in myself. I was drawn to Walter because he was an African-American male that had taken the same journey, and he could relate to every battle that I was facing. After meeting with Walter each week, I was more confident and able to experience college and the many benefits that it offered. Once my mindset and outlook changed, I was able to conquer the fear of the unknown and I knew that I could achieve great things.

. . . . . ● . . . . .

Progress takes perseverance. It is steadfastness in doing something despite difficulty. It means moving forward toward a destination despite what others think or say. I was the first in my family to graduate from college. I received my Bachelor of Arts degree on May 15, 1995 from Baylor University. This achievement was a testament to my desire, will, and drive. I often think about what I accomplished, despite the fact that people told me that I was not smart enough to go to college. People would tell me that college was not a possibility for me because my mother and father did not finish high school. Graduating from college was one of my greatest accomplishments because I persevered and truly defied the odds.

You have to be willing to defy the odds in order to move forward. According to some, I never should have made it to the National Football League. I was told that I was inadequate as an athlete. They told me that I was not big enough, strong enough, or fast enough, but the will to succeed in life will always supersede the negativity of others. Trust and believe in your own talents and persevere through all trials. If you are able to accomplish this, you will become a stronger individual, capable of great progress.

As you progress in life, you will have to endure many things along the path to achievement. However, no one achieves anything great in life without hardships and difficulty. To build the character necessary to progress toward your goal, perseverance is required. Throughout your journey you will be challenged, but your perseverance will allow you to overcome the challenges and make the progress needed to achieve your goals.

. . . . ● ● . . . .

Progress is raising the bar of achievement in order to maximize our opportunities. Raising the bar means asking, "What more can I do?" It is raising the standards in order to achieve greater results. It is very easy for us to do just enough to get by, to only do what we are asked, to not go above and beyond what is expected of us. But, in order to make great progress, you must be willing to do more and reach far beyond what is expected. I often ask myself, "What more I can do to make a difference in the lives of others?" Because I have made a commitment to be a change agent in this world, I constantly seek opportunities to raise the bar.

In the Fall of 2015, I was booked by the Community Relations Department at Syracuse University to do a speaking engagement at a Faith, Family, and Football event at Hendricks Hall. I was very excited about the opportunity to speak there because I enjoy speaking to college students about college life and beyond. A week before I was scheduled to fly to Syracuse, New York, I heard about the horrible acts of gun violence happening in the community right outside of the university. I immediately thought about how I could support the South Syracuse community, which had one the highest rates of extreme poverty in the country and a heavy concentration of Blacks and Hispanics. I spoke with Syeisha Byrd, the Director of Engagement Programs at Syracuse University and Johnathon Santiago, one of the campus chaplains, about doing a community event with the youth at one of the local Boys and Girls Clubs. They thought that it was extraordinary that I was willing to support the community, being that it was not directly connected with my previously booked engagement. I felt that it was my duty to support the community because of the growth (progress) that I had made in my life. I owed it to the community to support them in any way that I could.

I was grateful for the opportunity to speak hope and life into the lives of the young people that night. I entered the local Boys and Girls Club in the South Syracuse community at peace because I knew that everything I had experienced in life had prepared me for this moment to encourage, challenge, and give hope to the young faces before me. I know that I have to give back to schools and communities because I owe it to the youth of today. I was once in the same place as those youth, in need of guidance and direction along the way to becoming who I am today. Progress is all about coming full circle and realizing that there is still so much more to do in life.

* * * * ● ● ● * * * *

As I mentioned before, progress can be seen as "coming full circle" and as true inspiration based on the journey in one's life. Everybody's life is a journey, but the striking question is: "How does your life's journey play out?" We all plan to move forward in life, but are we truly willing to embrace the journey to make progress? I now can look back and see that the progress that means the most to me is not measured by financial or material gains, but by the lessons that I have learned throughout my journey. Being the first in my family to attend college is progress. Applying myself to my studies for four years is progress. Earning a degree in sociology from Baylor University is progress. Even though my NFL career was short lived, I realized that an education lasts a lifetime, another reflection of my progress. My mother and father were right in telling me that the greatest value in life would come from receiving my education. What I now know is that having a life rich with the wisdom amassed from experience is far superior to possessions and grand mansions. *Having a purpose in life worth striving for is the greatest reward.* As I look back over my life and think about the various things that I set out to do as a little boy, I see the reality of my hard work, perseverance, desire, and dedication as an adult, and I see progress.

It is sometimes very hard for us to see our progress. In this microwave society where technology is geared toward giving us immediate results, it can be challenging to remain committed to long-term goals. Sometimes we easily give up when we do not see the progress that we want to see when we want to see it. Progress can be measured based on your achievement of the desired goals that you have set for yourself. As you take a self-inventory of the various life goals that you have achieved, you can also monitor your progress by evaluating the various action items that you wish to accomplish. Are you making progress on the action items that you have committed to? Are you genuinely making strides to improve daily, weekly, and monthly based on what you have established for yourself? Overall, a true measure of progress is in knowing that you are being true to yourself while analyzing the effort that you put forth. Remember, your efforts will pay off. It may feel otherwise, but your effort is worthwhile. Throughout your journey you will understand why you have had failed experiences in the past, and you will know that in truth you have never failed. Your progress has required each one of those failures for you to get to where you are now. Just believe in yourself, believe in your dreams, and walk courageously toward your own goals. You will succeed, but you must always be willing to improve by setting new standards and goals for yourself. Never stop. Never settle. Keep growing. Keep learning. Keep achieving. Keep progressing.

* * * * * * * * * *

KEY POINT:

- ◆ When you are living out your goals and continuing to set new standards for yourself, you are making progress. Never settle for anything less.

KEY ACTION:

- ◆ Measure your progress knowing that you have given the pursuit of your dreams your absolute best efforts. Do the best that you can with the best that is within you, and you will never fail. You simply cannot fail.

"*Progress equals growth when you can look back and examine your personal growth and reflect on the changes that you have made.*"

- Tyrone Smith: Outside the Huddle

OUTSIDE *the* HUDDLE

Steps to Developing a Game Plan for Life

OUTSIDE *the* HUDDLE

Steps to Developing a Game Plan for Life

PAUSE

· · · · · ● · · · ·

"Sometimes in life a time-out is necessary."

- Tyrone Smith

Has there ever been a period in your life when you wanted to stop doing something or just take a break? Have you ever been so caught up in the moment that you completely lost sight of the fact that you have control over your life? Believe it or not, you do have control and something as simple as taking a pause in life helps us remain in control. Here is an example of why a pause is sometimes necessary for our progress.

As a kid, I always wanted to be a starting player on a

Division One college football team. By my third year in college at Baylor University, this dream became a reality. Coming out of spring football practice, I was announced as one of the starting cornerbacks and I was very excited. I truly felt that I had showcased my talent as one of the best defensive backs on the football team. I was anxious for the start of the upcoming season, but I had no idea what would happen during my first game. My first college game as a starting player at Baylor University was against Fresno State University, and the future Super Bowl Champion, Trent Dilfer, was the starting quarterback for Fresno State (multiple players on the Fresno state football team that year would eventually go on to play in the NFL). As I stepped onto the field I could feel my heart pounding in my throat as my stomach turned roller coaster style flips. I warmed up for the game and the tension of the moment prepared me. I felt focused and ready.

Fresno State won the coin toss and elected to receive the football, meaning that our defensive unit would take the field first. In those first moments after the coin toss my body felt paralyzed. My mind went blank and I forgot everything I had ever learned about the game of football. Truth be told, I couldn't have told you my own name in those first moments. I wanted to run away, go back to the locker room, clear my head, get a drink of water; yet none of those options were available to me. As we took the field, my mind was in a daze and we had not even called our first defensive play. I eventually came out of my state of paralysis and made it to the huddle to receive the defensive call; we then broke the huddle to prepare for the first play.

The quarterback shouted, "Down, set, hut!" When he said, "Hut," I blacked out. The next thing I can recall is getting up from tackling the wide receiver after he ran a quick curl route. Now remember that I said I *blacked out*. I do not remember backpedaling to defend the wide receiver on the quick curl route or even driving out of my backpedal to tackle the wide receiver. I was still very emotional, star struck, and just plain unstable because of the intensity of the moment. I got up and prepared for the second play, but I was still in the same mental state. I went back to the huddle to get the second defensive call, and a couple of my teammates asked if I was all right.

"Of course," I said. "I am good."

Second down . . . the quarterback yelled, "Down, set, hut!" When he said, "Hut," I froze and stood flat footed as the wide receiver ran toward me. He eventually ran right past me, so I turned to chase him while the quarterback dropped back and threw him the ball. He was wide open, and he dropped the ball for a clear touchdown. After Coach Reedy saw the way that I was playing, he called a time-out to immediately force a pause in the action. As I walked to the sideline, I did not see the same confidence in everyone's eyes I saw during spring practice. My coach challenged me to regroup and refocus because he knew that I was better than what I was showcasing at that moment. I needed that moment to regroup.

Sometimes in life we need to take a time-out to think through certain situations to see what adjustments we need to make. I really needed a time-out at that point in the game. In sports, a **time-out** is a halt in the play. This allows the coaches of either team to communicate with the team, in most cases to determine strategy or to inspire morale. It can also be used as a strategy to stop the game clock. A coach, player or referee can call a time-out.

To take a time-out or pause in life is necessary to reflect and review your current position. Just like in any sporting event, taking a time-out in life is necessary to ensure that you can make the best call or determine the best action at a particular moment. When you take a time-out in both sports and in life, it is most likely at a particular point when it is needed most. Think about your life for a moment and think about all of the tasks facing you. Are you at a place in life where you feel that you may need to pause? Do you need to pause because you are unsure of the path that your future may take? Do you need to pause some relationships? Do you need to pause some things in your life that may be a distraction, things that are keeping you from moving ahead in your life? A pause may be the best thing for you, but you have to be honest with yourself in order to recognize the necessity of taking a break. Taking an honest look at yourself will provide you with a point of evaluation for the areas in your life that may need change. It is not always easy to see that changes need to be made. When you pause, you are able to truly evaluate your life. You can reflect carefully and thoughtfully on your behaviors and beliefs. In doing so, you become more aware of yourself as an individual and of the areas in your life that may need further work.

> *When you pause and take a time-out, you can evaluate yourself and become willing to make a change.*
>
> *- Tyrone Smith*

· · · · **●** · · · ·

In middle school, I realized that I had to take a pause from a friend that was making a lot of bad decisions. We grew up together in our neighborhood and we often played together as kids. As we grew older and were preparing to go to middle school, he started doing things that I did not agree with. He started stealing bikes in the neighborhood and selling the parts. He also started stealing when we would go to the neighborhood store, and he eventually started using drugs. I knew that his behaviors and beliefs were not in line with my own, nor was his character or his personality similar to mine. I felt that the best thing for me to do at the time was to take an extended time-out from him. The day that I decided to remove myself from the friendship, I was transformed. I was able to realize that I had value as a person, and I did not need anyone else to validate who I am. However, I did not see this until I took a pause from the friendship. I personally made better decisions daily, and I truly felt better about myself because I was no longer surrounded by negative influences in the false form of a friendship. Taking a pause at this time in my life was crucial, because it helped me to step back and analyze a potentially dangerous situation.

Sometimes in life you need to pause or take a time-out when you feel pressured. It can be pressure that you put on yourself or pressure that others place on you. When I was a freshman at Baylor University, I would often put a lot of pressure on myself to succeed in college because I was the first in my family to attend. I did not want to let my family down. So, once a week I would take a pause and visit with my mentor, Walter Abercrombie. I would talk to Walter about the various issues and situations that I was dealing with because I was a first year and first generation college student. I was overwhelmed and needed this time to connect with someone about how I was feeling. Taking time to pause and break away from the new rigors of being a college student helped me in so many ways. There were times when I felt that I was not made for college, but the intentional pauses with Walter gave me an opportunity to regroup and refocus. To take a pause means to find ways that you can intentionally stop, regroup, and think things through.

During my freshman year in college, I also felt pressured by my peers. I felt that I had to keep up a certain image because I was on the football team, and I needed to do what my friends were doing to belong. I attended all of the parties with my teammates, not because I really enjoyed it, but because I felt it was what I needed to do to keep up appearances and be popular. I quickly learned that these parties were more trouble than fun for me. At nearly every party, there were often people there that didn't attend Baylor, and it seemed they liked to start trouble. They knew we had more to lose being members of the football team. At one party, I remember having to become involved in a fight to protect a group of young women that attended the party with us. One guy picked a fight with one of the young women, and very quickly an all-out brawl with several of them ensued. Because my teammates were involved, we all jumped in to protect one another and the young women. After fighting my way out and getting my group to safety, I had to take a moment to question if it was necessary for me to continue putting myself in these harmful situations. I soon realized that this wasn't something that I had to be involved in and it could possibly jeopardize my future. I needed to take a pause. I made the decision to disconnect from what others believed I should be doing, and focus on the things that I wanted to do and the person that I wanted to be. In situations like these, where it may be necessary to regroup and refocus, we can only achieve clarity when we pause.

· · · · ● ● ● · · · ·

Earlier in this chapter, I spoke about an important time-out that was taken my sophomore year during the football game against Fresno State. It was a high scoring football game and it came down to the wire. Fresno State was close to scoring one last time, and if they had scored they would have had the lead in the game. We took our final time-out, and our coach instructed everyone to be alert because the outcome of the game would depend on each of us defensively. Fresno State lined up for a scoring opportunity and the quarterback sounded out . . . "Down, set, hut."

The offensive play was run away from me to the opposite side of the field, and I proceeded to pursue from the backside. All of a sudden, the wide receiver handed the ball to another receiver, and he reversed field and headed for the end zone. I ran as fast as I could to get to the outside of the play in order to turn the play back inside to my fellow defensive players, who were in hunt and destruct mode. I quickly got to the outside and contained the play. Because of this, our linebacker was able obliterate the wide receiver. Our offense took possession of the ball, and we won the game. At the end of the game I was relaxed and focused, which allowed for me to make a big play to clinch the win for our team, but it was only because we took a time-out or pause earlier in the game. This pause allowed for me to regroup and focus on the actions that needed to be taken in order for me to perform on a high level.

On the path to achieving our goals and dreams, many times we need to take a time-out or pause from life in order to perform to the best of our abilities. These moments are just as important as taking action. They give us the right perspective about our thoughts, feelings, and actions, and will help us reflect on how far we have come and what we still need to do. It is crucial that you take these moments for yourself to evaluate and identify changes you need to make to improve your performance and your life. Take a deep breath and think. Pause and reflect. When you resume action, you will know why you stopped. These moments will give you clarity and the strength to pursue your dreams again.

* * * * ✹ ✹ ✹ * * *

KEY POINT:

♦ Taking a pause is necessary in life to ensure that you are able to make the best decisions for your life. Pausing gives us the right perception about our thoughts, feelings, and actions and will help us reflect on how far we have come and what we still need to do.

KEY ACTION:

♦ Pause so you can evaluate yourself and assess whether or not changes need to be made. Pausing is necessary to reflect and review where you are in life. Remember, taking a pause is just as important as taking action.

"Taking an honest look at yourself will provide you with a point of evaluation for the changes that need to be made in your life."

- Tyrone Smith: Outside the Huddle

OUTSIDE

the

HUDDLE

Steps to Developing a Game Plan for Life

OUTSIDE

the

HUDDLE

Steps to Developing a Game Plan for Life

CONCLUSION

"The time is always right to do what is right."

-Martin Luther King, Jr.

Because we have individual goals and aspirations, it is important to realize that each stage of our journeys will differ. We will pause and plan differently. We will practice and progress differently. We will encounter a different process and different people. We will also have different pitfalls and a different purpose. However, we are the same in that we each have the capacity to grow, the key to maintaining and sustaining our game plan for life. When I reflect on the struggles that I have fought through in life, I wonder, "How did I get this far?" The answer is simple—my life experiences allowed me to understand that life is filled with many obstacles and opportunities, but the ultimate challenge is learning how to grow from these experiences. I truly can say that I have grown as an individual from the different experiences that I have encountered, and I trust that each reader will be able to learn from the life lessons presented in this book and to apply the knowledge to their own life.

> *"Destiny is not a matter of chance, it is a matter of choice; it is not a thing to be waited for, it is a thing to be achieved."*
>
> *-Winston Churchill*

For me, saying that I have obtained success in life is too finite a statement. I do not believe that success is a fixed destination; instead, once one goal is achieved, we should strive to reach new heights. I hope that this book has motivated you to create steps to develop a game plan for your life, but more than that, I hope that in reading this book you will see the value of believing in yourself and in your dreams. You have unique abilities, skills, and talents, and now is the time to maximize all that makes you who you are and to focus on striving to reach your dreams. Most importantly, believing that you are able to achieve greatness is at the core of each step. I once believed that my place in life was on the football field, but I ultimately found my true purpose, *outside the huddle*. It does not matter about one's color, neighborhood, belief, background, social or economic status when it comes to believing and trusting in one's self. We all have value and the capacity to make a difference. You can achieve greatness if you put your mind to it and prepare yourself to succeed each day, regardless of the barriers before you. Do not be afraid to step *outside the huddle* in your own life.

"Now is the time to maximize all that makes you who you are and to focus on striving to reach your dreams."

- Tyrone Smith

OUTSIDE
the
HUDDLE

ACKNOWLEDGEMENTS

This book would not have been possible without the prayers, support and encouragement of my wife, DeMonica Smith. She has been instrumental in my growth to strive beyond my limits as a husband, father and youth advocate. I would like to thank my parents, Jettie and Harold Smith, for bringing me into this world and for the countless sacrifices they made for Tusshun, Harold, Jr. and myself. Both of my parents have always been driven, dedicated hard workers, and I can say that I received my determination from them. To my loving children, Whitney, Tyrone II and Tyler Smith, you all are an inspiration and motivation. I am genuinely and forever grateful to Patricia Landheart for finding a place for me in her heart as a son and for making such a great sacrifice for me. I am thankful to my in-laws, Patricia Leeks and Maurice Davis. They have always supported me throughout my career and also supported me with authoring this book. Words cannot express my gratitude for my sister-in-law, Darla Dawkins, for wanting to help tell my story to the world because of her fascination with my passion to serve and support others. To all of my family members from Jasper, Texas and Houston, Texas, you have always been my truest fans and supportive of all that I have done in life.

I am truly thankful to my pastor, Dr. Ralph Douglas West, who has been a great influence in my life since I became a member of The Church Without Walls as a sophomore in college. His life is a pure example of true leadership, drive and a genuine desire to live a life for Christ. Not only do I refer to him as my pastor, but I also can say that he is a friend. Through all of the experiences of life and the challenges that I have faced, he has always been a source of encouragement, wisdom and sound teaching. I will always appreciate and cherish his influence and impact on my life. I also would like to thank the Church Without Walls family, who have supported me throughout the years.

To my coach and friend, Coach Dennis Brantley, thanks for always being a true support in my life. Your influence and leadership in my life have empowered me to strive to be a better version of myself. Your character and encouragement have always challenged me to be a true example in the lives of all the people that I have connected with over time.

A true mentor is someone that can guide, challenge, connect and teach in a way that one feels empowered to take on the challenges of life. I am grateful for one of my mentors, Walter Abercrombie, for being an example of excellence.

Thank you for supporting me through one of my greatest transitions in life. When I came to Baylor University I was an unsure young man; I left with a greater sense of confidence and purpose because of your impact on my life.

To my friend and brother in Christ, Pastor Allen Rice, thank you for encouraging me, championing me, and holding me accountable. Your friendship and brotherhood have been a true blessing to my life.

To the Fellowship of Christian Athletes organization, thank you for making such a great impact on my life as early as the eighth grade. I was a shy, young man that lacked confidence, but the Fellowship of Christian Athletes helped empower me for the life that I would live for Christ.

I truly appreciate Lee "L.A." Warren, Derek Smith, Cora Alexander, Dr. Andriel Brice, Erica L. James, Rachel Fogg, Kiffany Dugger and Enid Henderson for their professional advice and assistance with this manuscript. I would also like to thank Joe Edmonson and Joel "Chap" Edmonson for always being available to use their gifts of graphic design, media and photography to support me over the years.

I am grateful for the educational institutions that have helped shaped who I am as a person. I would like to thank the administration and staff of Parnell Elementary, Turner Elementary, Ridgemont Elementary, Missouri City Middle School, Christa McAuliffe Middle School, Willowridge High School and Baylor University. Thanks to all of my coaches, teammates and teachers who pushed me to become better. The journey that I have taken has not been an easy one, but you encouraged and supported me along the way.

Much love to my family and friends for sharing my happiness when starting this project and for your continued encouragement when it seemed too difficult to complete. I am humbled and grateful for all who supported and encouraged me throughout this journey to make this dream become a reality.

To all of the students whose lives I have impacted— continue to lead, love others and give back.

Made in the USA
Charleston, SC
02 November 2016